Workbook
for Learning Elementary Arabic 101

الكِتاب المُسَاعِد في تَعْليم اللُّغَةِ العَرَبِيَّة لِلْمُسْتَوى الإبْتِدَائي

Siham Eldadah, M.A.

Copyright © 2024 by – Siham Eldadah – All Rights Reserved

It is illegal to reproduce, duplicate, or transmit any part of this document in either electronic means or printed format. Recording of this publication is strictly prohibited.

About the Author

الكِتابُ ألمُسَاعِدُ في تَعْليمِ الْلُّغَةِ العَرَبِيَّةِ للمُسْتَوى الإبْتِدَائِي

Siham Sharif Eldadah, MA, has taught Arabic language and culture to English-speaking students for decades including the past 14 years teaching at Montgomery College, Rockville, Maryland, and other higher education students. This workbook grew out of her classroom lessons both in person and virtual.

The sections in the Workbook For Learning Arabic 101 are presented in a simple format intended for beginners without prior knowledge of the Arabic language. English transliteration of Arabic letters and comparable meanings of words enable a steady pace of learning to master correct pronunciation by applying the vowels (markers) with each letter. In some examples and exercises, the learner is given the opportunity to figure out the pronunciation of each letter in repeated words without vowels and fill in the correct ones.

Siham hopes that this workbook will help students of all ages and backgrounds learn this rich and exquisite language.

Table of Contents

Dedication الأهداء 6

Acknowledgement تقدير 7

Introduction 8

Table 1 Arabic Letters 10

Section I: Sets of Letter Forms and Sounds 11

Section II: Vowel Sounds 18

Section III: Listening to Sounds 28

Section IV: Connections of Letters 42

Section V: Vocabulary 83

Section VI: Interrogatives and Prepositions 91

Section VII: Noun and Pronoun 117

Section VIII: Adjectives الصِّفات "assifat" 146

Section IX: Idafa Phrase 171

Section X: The Nominal (Noun) Sentence 181

Section XI: The Verb Sentence 203

Section XII: Base letters and Patterns 235

Section XIII: Arabic Vocabulary Puzzles 1-1 to 8-1 257

Section XIV: Appendices 265

    Appendix 1: Commonly Used Nouns 265

    Appendix 2-A: Commonly Used Masculine Verbs 273

    Appendix 2-B: Commonly Used Feminine Verbs 280

    Appendix 3: Standard Conjugation of the Past Verb 287

    Appendix 4: Standard Conjugation of the Present Verb 290

    Appendix 5: Commonly Used Adjectives 294

    Appendix 6: Commonly used Opposite Adjectives 298

    Appendix 7: Commonly Used Adjective Phrases 301

    Appendix 8: Commonly Used Idafa Phrases 304

    Appendix 9: Commonly Used Colors 307

    Appendix 10: Commonly Used Prepositions and Adverbs 309

    Appendix 11: Most Commonly Attached Pronoun Suffixes to Prepositions and Adverbs 310

Appendix 12: Commonly Used Preposition and Adverb Phrases 312

Appendix 13: Commonly Used Particles 315

Appendix 14: Answers for Arabic vocabulary puzzles 1-1 to 8-1 317

List of Recommended Resources 325

Dedication   الإهداء

In loving memory of Dr. Adnan H. Eldadah

Acknowledgement تقدير

My students and friends who have sought to learn and improve their Arabic have given me deep inspiration to produce this book. And, of course, Arabic itself is a language that I love, inspires me to share it with passion.

I am very grateful to Dr. Angela Lanier, who has partnered with me from the very start in producing the *Workbook for Learning Arabic 101*. Working with Angela has been a true joy and an unforgettable collaboration.

Profound gratitude goes to many members of my family, who encouraged me and helped refine this workbook with their reviews, edits, and constructive comments. They include Drs. Zayd and Basil Eldadah, Mona Eldadah, and Samaa Eldadah. Deep thanks go to Dr. Mithal Albassam and Muna Omeri, who enhanced this book with numerous helpful ideas.

Special thanks also go to Mustafa Sharif for his expert computer skills, especially Arabic Microsoft Word. I am indebted to Mercedes Ovalle, who created the book's original graphic art.

I am especially thankful to Ruth Rivers who initiated the publication process. My gratitude to Zara Morton, Harvey West, Nate Reese, and all their teams together with the design team. This workbook would not have come to be without their dedicated support, and tireless help along with the rest of the staff at Amazon Publishing Pros.

Bringing this labor of love to fruition would not have been possible without the help and support from all of you. My appreciation is immense and perpetual. Responsibility for any inadequacies in the workbook rests with me.

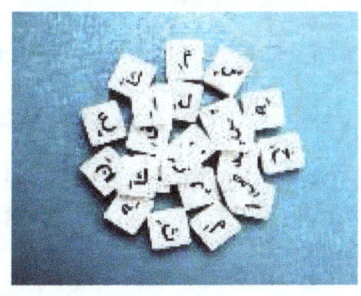

Introduction

This workbook is intended for instructors or learners of the Arabic language. The purpose is to support the pronunciation, reading, writing, listening, and comprehension of students learning elementary-level Arabic 101. Students often comment that beginners need to practice with the letters and sounds to help them build a strong foundation in the early stages of their learning. To provide instructors with tools to facilitate student learning and address this challenge, this workbook is a collection of exercises for use in class or out-of-class practice.

In creating this workbook, the emphasis was on building a collection of audio-lingual exercises as a starting point to help the learner or instructor assess learners' basic knowledge. They will find readily available exercises that emphasize the sounds of letters and their shapes. This will save time that may be used for other creative instruction. Following the audio-lingual practice, the instructor or learner can proceed with the application of Arabic letters at a gradually advancing pace.

This workbook contains 12 sections. Each section has two parts. The first part offers detailed instructions and examples of the skill, and the second part includes exercises that can be used for practice or tests. For each section, both vocabulary and gender are emphasized. Section 13 is a practice of Arabic vocabulary puzzles. Section 14 is commonly used vocabulary. As vocabulary is mastered and memorized, it will become easier for students to construct sentences and allow the instructors to spend more time on grammatical structure. As listening and reading skills improve, comprehension slowly develops. At this point, learners begin engaging themselves with passages, either in groups or through one-on-one interaction.

We emphasize again that the exercises are templates to select from and adapt to serve the learners based on the skills/content they need to learn.

This workbook is designed as a supplement to Arabic 101 textbooks, and to support the instructor in guiding and assessing student learning.

As you use this workbook, please note the following:

- Some Arabic words do not have an exact English equivalent. All translations of any Arabic words are as close as possible to an English word with a similar meaning.
- Every Arabic word, except articles, is either masculine or feminine. Masculine words are noted with the initial 'm' and feminine words are noted with the initial 'f' next to the transliteration or English translation. Other notations of 'm' or 'f' are indicated in the texts of every section.
- All the images were created by Mercedes Ovalle, the Graphic artist, using digital graphic imaging software.
- The following abbreviations are used throughout the workbook:

f	Feminine
m	Masculine
fs	Feminine singular
ms	Masculine singular
fp	Feminine plural
mp	Masculine plural
f-m,p	Feminine/masculine plural
b	Broken plural
bmp	Broken masculine plural
bfp	Broken feminine plural
s	Sound plural
msp	Masculine sound plural
fsp	Feminine sound plural
r	Regular
irr	Irregular
irrp	Irregular plural
ل	Written but not pronounced

Table 1 Arabic Letters
الحُرُوف العَرَبِيَّة

(*) **No comparable English letter-sound**

ذ	د	خ	ح	ج	ث	ت	ب	ا
THE	D	*	*	J	*	T	B	A
ع	ظ	ط	ض	ص	ش	س	ز	ر
*	*	*	*	SOD	SH	S	Z	R
و	ه	ن	م	ل	ك	ق	ف	غ
W	H	N	M	L	K	*	F	*
			ء	لا	لا	ىٰ	ي
			EH	LA	LA	as <u>AA</u>	Y

Section I: Sets of Letter Forms and Sounds

First Set of Letters:

Form of Arabic Letter	Transliterated name of Arabic letter	English Letter w/ comparable Sound	Arabic sound in English
ا	alif	a	**Eh**
ب	baa'	b	**b**oy
ت	taa'	t	**t**ight
ج	jeem	g/j	**G**eorge/**j**am
د	dal	d	**d**ad
ر	raa'	r	**r**ight
ز	zaa'	z	**z**ebra
س	seen	s	**s**ight

Second Set of Letters:

Form of Arabic Letter	Transliterated name of Arabic letter	English Letter w/ comparable Sound	Arabic sound in English
ف	faa'	f	**f**at
ك	kaaf	k	**k**ite
ل	laam	l	**l**it
م	meem	m	**m**ight
ن	noon	n	**n**ight
ه‍	haa'	H	**h**at
و	wow	w	**w**ire
ي	yaa'	y	**y**es
ء	hamza	eh	**I**t
ى	alif maqsooreh	ah	**A**nne
لا or لا	lam alif	la	**la**mb

Third Set of Letters:

Form of Arabic Letter	Transliterated name of the Arabic letter	English Letter w/ comparable Sound	Arabic sound in English
ث	thaw'	Thea	**th**umb
ذ	thal	the	**th**ere
ش	sheen	Sh	**sh**ip

Fourth Set of Letters:

Form of Arabic Letter	Transliterated name of Arabic letter	English Letter w/ comparable Sound	Arabic sound in English
ح	deep sound ha'	*	*
خ	kha'	*	*
ص	sod	*	*
ض	dhad	*	*
ط	*	**T**okyo	**T**okyo
ظ	*	*	*
ع	*	*	*
غ	*	*	*
ق	qaf	*	*

Note: Boxes with (*) indicate the letters that do not have English equivalent sounds. The instructor is encouraged to demonstrate the correct sound and pronunciation of these letters. (Review pages 13-14.)

Fourth Set of Letters

The following nine (9) Arabic letters have no comparable English sounds:

ق   غ   ع   ظ   ط   ض   ص   خ   ح

To produce the right sound of each of these letters, the student is encouraged to associate the sound of the letter with the coordinated muscles of the mouth and throat and clenching of the teeth together with an image to remind the student of the sound.

For a beginner, it may take longer to remember each sound. Combining these letters with others in a word will help the student to retain the sound of the letter in question. However, mastering these sounds depends on support from the instructor and available media to train students in the production.

The following description of these 9 letter sounds is an attempt to ease the challenges that a student may encounter. The examples are the closest sounds to the Arabic sounds:

- "ح" Heavy sound from the back of the throat such as **Hay**at (حَيَاة 'f') which means *life* in Arabic.

- "خ" The sound is made at the back of the palate of the mouth such as the **kh** in **kh**eber (خَبَر 'm') which means *news*. It might remind you of the sound of someone snoring!

- "ص" The sound is made at the back of the palate of the mouth with the clenched teeth as in **S**od which means *grass surface piece.*

- "ض" A sound produced from the back of the teeth and back of the throat such as a strong emphatic sound as in **day**yiq (ضَيِّق 'm') which means *tight*.

- "ط" sounds similar to the combination of the first two letters of the capital of Japan, **To**kyo (طُوكيُو 'f') or **tay**r (طَيْر 'm') which means *bird*.

13

- "ظ" makes the emphatic sound of "the" by curving your tongue in front of your front teeth as if you are cupping them. In Arabic **thaa**her (ظَـاهِـر 'm') which means *obvious*.

- "ع" emphatic guttural sound of **iy** as in Arabic **iy**en (عَـيْـن 'f') which means *eye*.

- "غ" emphatic sound from the back of the throat **gh** similar to **gu** in **gu**ru or as in Arabic **gh**erb (غَـرْب 'm') which means *west*.

- "ق" is a sound produced between the back of the tongue and the pharynx as in Arabic **qe**deem (قَـدِيـم 'm') which means *old*.

Notes:

Test I-1: Letter Forms, Names, and Sounds

I-1. Write the number of each transliterated Arabic name from Column 1 next to its corresponding Arabic letter form in Column 2.

1 Transliterated Arabic names	2 Arabic letter forms
1. alif	ر
2. baa	س
3. sod	ا
4. noon	هـ / ه
5. sheen	ب
6. haa	ذ
7. raa	ص
8. kaaf	ن
9. thal	ش
10. seen	ك

I-2. Circle the Arabic letter that corresponds to a letter sound in each English word. Underline the English letter that corresponds to the Arabic letter you select.

1. red	م	ش	ر	6. way	ذ	و	ز	
2. sun	د	س	ت	7. bat	ب	ظ	ح	
3. mop	ك	ث	م	8. jay	خ	م	ج	
4. not	ه، ة	ن	ع	9. wheat	ط	و	ب	
5. take	ا	ف	ت	10. yes	ي	غ	ق	

I-3. Fill in each blank with the Arabic letter that matches the sound of each of the following English letters:

1- R _____   2- M _____   3- W _____   4- Sh _____   5- H _____

6- N _____   7- K _____   8- F _____   9- L _____   10- D _____

I-4. Which Arabic letter sound is the same as the <u>beginning</u> sound in each English word? On the line, write the Arabic letter that matches the beginning sound.

1. top _____   6. thin _____

2. the _____   7. bay _____

3. yellow _____   8. second _____

4. jam _____   9. big _____

5. fear _____   10. zoo _____

Notes:

Section II: Vowel Sounds

Basic Short Vowel Sounds
Long Vowel Sounds
Derived Vowel Sounds (Attanween)
Sukoon, Shadda, Meddeh, and Wasleh Sounds

Every letter in Arabic words carries **a vowel**.

Basic Short Vowel Sound:

- **FatHa** (فَ تْ حَ ة) with the sound of (e) in **et**.

- **Kasra** (كَ سْ رَ ة) with the sound of (i) in **it**.

- **Damma** (ضَ مَّ ة) with the sound of (u) in p**u**t.

The FatHa is a short dash above the letter (‾ .) Kasra is a short dash at the bottom of the letter (_), and Damma is a small comma-like (ُ) on top of the letter.

Examples:

The letter ب with a FatHa is بَ (be), with a Kasra is بِ (bi), and with a Damma it is بُ (bu.)

A long Vowel Sound is an elongated basic vowel sound placed on the letter regardless of its position in the word:

- **The long sound FatHa** is consonant with default FatHa when followed by the letter ا (alif.) The **long sound Kasra** is the consonant with a default Kasra when followed by the letter ي (yaa'), and the **long sound Damma** is the consonant with a default Damma followed by the letter و (waw.)

Examples: بَ ا (baa)

بِ ي (bii/bee)

بُ و (boo)

- When the letter (ا) is at the beginning of the word followed by و or ي the basic vowel sound, FatHa is the dominant one.
- When the letter (ي) is prefixed by a consonant with FatHa, the basic vowel sound FatHa is the dominant one.
- When a consonant prefixes the letter (و) with FatHa, the basic vowel sound FatHa is the dominant one.

Examples: أَيْ 'ay'   أَوْ 'aw'
 بَيْ 'bay'   سَيْ 'say'
 بَوْ 'beaw'   جَوْ 'jeaw'

Derived vowel sounds (Attanween -Nunation) الـ تً و ي نْ are the double basic vowel added to letters. They produce the following sounds:
- Tanween of FatHa sound is **un,** for example, the word (fun.) It is always placed on top of the (ا) suffixed ending of a consonant.
- Tanween of Kasra is the sound **in,** for example, the word (thin.) It is always placed at the bottom of the consonant.
- Tanween of Damma is **une,** for example, the word (tune.) It is always placed on top of the consonant.

Examples: بًا (bun - babun)   بَابًا door

 بٍ (bin - babin)   بَابٍ

 بٌ (bune - babune)   بَابٌ

Sukoon (silent sound) is a tiny circle o marker that does not change the sound of the consonant in a word. Because Sukoon does not affect the sound of a consonant, it may or may not be placed on top of that letter.

Examples: بْ (be)   تْ (te)

Shadda is a vowel with the shape of a tiny w that acts similar to an accent mark. The presence of the vowel w indicates stress in the sound of the letter. It is always placed on top of the letter and under its basic vowel FatHa or Damma. The Kasra is placed under the Shadda or the letter.

Examples: Shadda Fat'Ha   بَّ   (bbe)

                  Shadda Kasra   بِّ or بّ   (bbi)

                  Shadda Damma   بُّ   (bbu)

The **Shadda** is necessary for the correct pronunciation of specific letters at the beginning of words prefixed with ال. Arabic letters are divided into two sets. Each set includes 14 letters. The first set is **Sun letters or Solar letters**:

حُرُوْف شَمْسِيَّة (huroof - shemsiyyeh.) These letters are:

ت ث د ذ ر ز س ش ص ض ط ظ ل ن

Shadda is placed on top of each solar letter when it follows the definite prefix ال (alif lam). These two letters define the nouns and adjectives. It is comparable in its use to the definite English article "the." When a sun letter is prefixed by ال the ا pronounces, and the ل is written with Sukoon but not pronounced. Shadda then is placed on top of the sun letter that follows.

Examples: the lesson   (a**dd**ers)   الْ دَّ رْس

               the car   (a**ss**ayyareh)   الْ سَّ يَّ ا رَ ة

               the figs   (a**tt**een)   الْ تِّ يْ ن

               the sunrise   (a**shsh**urooq)   الْ شُّ رُو ق

The second set of letters is **Moon Letters or Lunar letters**:

حُرُوف قَمَرِيَة (huroof - qemeriyyeh). These letters are:

أ ب ج ح خ ع غ ف ق ك م هـ و ي

When ال prefixes a moon letter, all the letters are pronounced clearly with a Sukoon on ل.

Examples:	the earth (alerdh)	اَلْ أَرْض
	the work (alamel)	اَلْ عَ مَ ل
	the homework (alwaajib)	اَلْ وَ ا جِ ب
	the book (alkitaab)	اَلْ كِ تَ ا ب

The **Madda** is a short wavy dash (~) added on top of Alif (آ .) It elongates the sound of Alif at the beginning, within, or at the end of the word,

Examples:	Adam (**Aa**dam)	آ دَ م
	Amen (**Aa**miin/ **Aa**meen)	آ مِ يْ ن
	August (**Aa**b)	آ ب
	Wells (**Aa**bar)	آ بَ آ ر
	Antiquities (**Aa**thar)	آ ثَ آ ر
	Now (Al**aa**n)	اَ لْ آ ن
	Full (Mel**aa**n)	مَ لْ آ ن

The **Wasla** is a tiny letter like (ﺻ) placed on top of the letter (أ) in a word that begins with أل and precedes by another word to muffle its sound and connects the sound of the last letter of the precedent word to ل (ٱ)

Examples:

the house door (baab-**ul**bayt) بَ ا بُ ٱلْ بَ يْ ت

the school teacher (ustaath-**ul**madraseh) أُسْ تَ ا ذُ ٱلْ مَ دْ رَ سَ ة

the scientist book (kitaaab-**ul**aalim) كِ تَ ا بُ ٱلْ عَ ا لِ م

Notes:

Test II: Vowels

II-1. Read each transliteration. Identify the Arabic short vowel sound in the underlined part of the transliteration. Then on the Arabic letter, **write** the vowel (FatHa, Kasra, Damma) that corresponds to the underlined sound.

1. Th<u>e</u>   ذ

2. M<u>u</u>   م

3. S<u>i</u>   س

4. T<u>i</u>   ت

5. N<u>e</u>   ن

6. R<u>i</u>   ر

7. W<u>e</u>   و

8. W<u>i</u>   و

9. Sh<u>i</u>   ش

10. K<u>i</u>   ك

11. K<u>e</u>   ك

12. K<u>u</u>   ك

II-2. Read the letter combination. Then **write** the appropriate long vowel on the first letter based on the letter that follows it.

1. خ و

2. م و

3. ا ذ

4. ا ب

5. ر ي

6. د و

7. م ا

8. ظ ي

9. ب ي

10. ح ي

11. ق و

12. ا خ

II-3. Add Tanween (double FatHa, double Kasra, and double Damma) on the last letter of the following Arabic words.

Double FatHa

	شُ كْ رَ ا	Shukr<u>un</u> (Thanks)
	عَ فْ وَ ا	Afw<u>un</u> (pardon me, you are welcome)
	مَ رْ حَ بَ ا	Merhab<u>un</u> (welcome)
	فِ عْ لَ ا	Fi'el<u>un</u> (indeed)
	جِ دَّ ا	Jidd<u>un</u> (very)
	أَهْـ لَ ا وَ سَ هْـ لَ ا	Ahl<u>un</u> weh sehl<u>un</u> (welcome, welcome)

Double Kasra

	سَ ا عَ ة	saa'et<u>in</u> (an hour 'f')
	كِ تَ ا ب	kitaab<u>in</u> (book 'm')
	كُ لِّ يَّ ة	kulliyet<u>in</u> (College 'f')
	سَ يَّ ا رَ ة	sayyaaret<u>in</u> (car 'f')

Double Damma

	مُ دَ رِّ سَ ة	muderriset<u>une</u> (teacher 'f')
	قَ لَ م	qelem<u>une</u> (pencil 'm')
	سَ مَ كَ ة	semeket<u>une</u> (fish 'f')
	شَ رِ يْ ف	Shariif<u>une</u>/ Shareef<u>une</u> (noble 'm')

II-4. Underline the letters in the transliteration that correspond to the **Sun letter-Shadda sound**. Then place the **Shadda** AND its appropriate **vowel** on the corresponding letter in each Arabic word.

ا ل س ي ّ ا رَ ة	1. asseyyaareh (the car 'f')
ا ل ز يْ ت	2. azzayt (the oil 'm')
ا ل ت ِمْ ثَ ا ل	3. attimthaal (the statue 'm')
ا ل ر ز	4. arruz (the rice 'm')
ا ل ن ا ر	5. annaar (the fire 'f')
ا ل س ف ِ يْ نَ ة	6. assefiineh (the vessel 'f')
ا ل ن ا َ ب ا	7. annebaat (the plant 'm')
ا ل ش ب ا ك	8. ashshubbaak (the window 'm')
ا ل د يْ ك	9. addeek/ addiik (the rooster 'm')
ا ل ن مْ ر	10. annimr (the tiger 'm')
ا ل س َ ع ا دَ ة	11. asseAdeh (the happiness 'f')
ا ل ر ب ي ع	12. arrebee' (the happiness 'f')
ا ل د ر ُوْ س	13. adduroos the (the lessons 'fp')
ا ل س لَ ا م	14. assalaam (the peace 'm')
ا ل ت مْ ر ِ يْ ن	15. attemreen/attemriin (the drill 'm')

Notes:

Section III: Listening to Sounds

Table 1. There are 28 Arabic letter sounds. Sixteen (16) of these sounds are comparable to English letter sounds.

English letter-sound	Arabic letter name, sound & form	transliteration of Arabic letter sound in an Arabic word *	English translation
A	Alif ا ، **Hamza ء on ا أ إ أ	أَ خ ekh 'm', إِ بْ ن ibn 'm', أُ خ ت ukht 'f'	brother, son, sister
B	Baa' ب	بَ يْ ت bayt 'm'	house
T	Taa' ت، ة	تُ وْ ت toot 'm'	mulberry
J, G	Jeem ج	جُ و رْ ج George, جَ مَ ل jemel 'm'	camel
D	Dal د	دَ ا ر daar 'f'	house
R	Raa' ر	رَ فِ يْ ق refeeq 'm'	companion
Z	Zaa' ز	زَ يْ ت zayt 'm'	oil
S	Seen س	سَ رَ ا ب seraab 'm'	mirage
F	Faa' ف	فِ ي لْ م fiilm 'm'	film
K	Kaf ك	كَ رِ يْ م kereem 'm'	generous
L	Lam ل	لَ هْـ/ةَ جَ ة lehjeh 'f'	dialect
M	Meem م	مَ سَ ا ء mesaa' 'm'	evening
N	Noon ن	نَ ا ر naar 'f'	fire
H	Haa' هـ، ة	هَـ/ةَ وَ ا ء hewaa' 'm'	air
W	Waw و	وَ قْ ت wehqt 'm'	time
Y	Yaa' ي	يَ وْ م yawm 'm'	day

** Hamza is always on top of alif with the vowel FatHa or damma. Hamza is always at the bottom of alif with the vowel Kasra. (Review pages 45-47.)

Table 2. Four (4) of the Arabic letter - sounds are comparable to a combination of two English letter - sounds

English letter-sound	Arabic letter name, sound & form	English word with the sound at the beginning	transliteration of Arabic letter sound in an Arabic word*	English translation
TH	thaa' ث	**TH**ing	ثَ مَرْ themer 'm'	fruit
SH	sheen ش	**SH**ip	شَ مْ سْ shems 'f'	sun
TH	thal ذ	**TH**is	ذَ هَـ/ةَ بْ theheb 'm'	gold
SA/SO	SA/SO ص	**SA**lt/**SO**d	صَ يْ فْ sayf 'm'	summer

*Memorize English transliterations and their meanings in tables 1-2 for better pronunciation.

Table 3. No comparable English letter - sounds for nine (9) Arabic letters:

Form of Arabic Letter	*English Letter w/no comparable Arabic sound* *
ح	*deep sound ha'*
خ	*none*
ص	*none*
ض	*none*
ط	*none*
ظ	*none*
ع	*none*
غ	*none*
ق	*none*

* **Review (p. 13-14)**

Notes:

Test III: Listening to Sounds

III-1. Listen and fill in the blanks with the missing letters you hear. Add the vowels:

Assistant's copy (Pronounce the words slowly and repeat if needed)

1. أ ــــ ي	my father 'm'	1. أبي
2. س ــــ ر ــــ ا	Syria 'f'	2. سوريا
3. م ــــ ت	death 'm'	3. موت
4. ــــ ؤا ــــ	question 'm'	4. سُؤَال
5. أ ــــ ت ي	my sister 'f'	5. أُختي
6. ــــ ش ــــ ر ــــ	tree 'f'	6. شجرة
7. ن ــــ ار	daytime 'm'	7. نهار
8. غ ــــ ــــ ة	room 'f'	8. غرفة
9. و ــــ ج ــــ	duty, homework 'm'	9. واجب
10. م ــــ ت ــــ	office 'm'	10 مكتب
11. ج ــــ د	good 'm'	11. جيّد
12. ب ــــ ا ي ــــ	building 'f'	12. بناية
13... ــــ ت ا ــــ ي	my teacher 'm'	13. أُستاذي
14. خ ــــ ــــ	bread 'm'	14. خبز

III-1.1 Fill in the blanks with the missing letters you hear. Add the vowels. Memorize the meaning:

Learner's copy

my father 'm'	1. أ ــــ ي
Syria 'f'	2. س ــــ ر ــــ ا
death 'm'	3. مَ ــــ ت
question 'm'	4. ــــ ؤ ا ــــ
my sister 'f'	5. أُ ــــ تِ ي
tree 'f'	6. ش ــــ رَ ــــ
daytime 'm'	7. ن ــــ ا ر
room 'f'	8. غ ــــ ــــ ة
duty, homework 'm'	9. و ــــ جِ ــــ
office 'm'	10. مَ ــــ ت ــــ
good 'm'	11. ج ــــ د
building 'f'	12. ــــ بِ ــــ ا يَ ــــ
my teacher 'm'	13. أُ ــــ ت ا ــــ ي
bread 'm'	14. خ ــــ ــــ

III-2. Listen to each phrase or sentence. Fill in the blanks with the missing letters you hear. Note to the assistant - repeat slowly the words 2-3 times:

Assistant's copy

1. هٰـذا كتاب أخي.	1. هٰـذا كـتـاب أ ـخ ـي .
2. البيت بعيد.	2. الـبـيـت بـعـيـد .
3. هٰـذِهِ أختي سمر.	3. هٰـذِهِ أُخـتـي سمر
4. هٰـذا الحِصّان أبْيَض.	4. هـذا الـحـصـان أبـيـض .
5. هٰـذِهِ وردة حمراء.	5. هـذه وردة حمـراء .
6. هو طالب في مدرسة عامّة.	6. هـو طـالـب فـي مـدرسـة عامّة .
7. هٰـذا قلم أُمّي.	7. هـذا قـلـم أُمـي .
8. هٰـذا صف اللُّغة العربية.	8. هـذا صـف الـلـغـة الـعـربـيـة .
9. أين تدرس يا سمير؟	9. أيـن تـدرس يـا سـمـيـر ؟

10. أنا أدرس في كلية.	10. أنا أ ـ ـ س ف ي ـ ـ ل ـ ـ ة.
11. أنا مهندس.	11. أنا م ـ ـ ن ـ ـ ـ.
12. أنت لبناني.	12. أنت ـ ـ ب ـ ـ ن ـ ـ ي.
13. سمير مدرس سوري.	13. س م ـ ر م د ـ ـ س ـ ـ و ـ ـ.
14. مع السلامة	14. م ع ال ـ ـ ل ـ م ـ ـ.
15. أنتم سودانيون.	15. أن ت م ـ ـ و ـ ـ ن ـ و ـ.
16. هو موظف.	16. هـ و م ـ ـ ظ ـ ـ.
17. أنت لبنانية.	17. أنت ل ـ ن ـ ن ـ ـ ـ.
18. أنا مصرية.	18. أن ا م ـ ـ ري ـ.
19. أنا أُسْتاذ في الجامعة.	19. أن ا أ س ـ ـ ذ ف ي ال ـ ا ـ ـ ـ ة.
20. هي طالبة في الكلية.	20. هـ ـ ـ ط ـ ل ب ـ ـ ف ي ال ـ ل ـ ـ ة.

III-2.2 Listen to each phrase or sentence. Fill in the blanks with the missing letters you hear. Note to Assistant - Repeat slowly the words 2-3 times:

Learner's copy

1. هٰـ ـا كـ ـتـ ـب أ ـ ـ ـ .
2. الـ ـتـ ـ ـ بـ ـ ي ـ .
3. هٰـ ذ ـ أُ ـ تـ ـ ـ س مر
4. ـ ذا الـ ـ ص ـ ن أ ـ ـ ض.
5. ـ ذه و ـ د ـ ـ ح م ـ ـ ء.
6. هـو ا ـ ـ ـ فـ ـ م ـ ر ـ ـ ة عامَّة.
7. ـ ذا ـ ـ م ـ ـ أ ـ ـ ـ .
8. ـ ـ ا ـ ص ـ ـ ة الـ ـ ـ ر ـ ي ة.
9. أ ـ ن تـ ـ ر س ياسـ ـ ي ر؟

10. أنـا أ ســس ف ي ل ــة.

11. أنا م ــن ــ.

12. أنت ــ ب ــ ن ي.

13. س م ــر م د ــ ــ و ــ ــ.

14. م ع ال ــ ل م ــ.

15. أن ت م ــ و ــ ن و ــ.

16. ه و م ــ ظ ــ.

17. أنت ل ــ ن ن ــ.

18. أ ن ا م ــ ري ــ.

19. أ ن ا أُ س ــ ذ ف ي ال ــ ا ــ ة.

20. ه ــ ط ــ ل ب ــ ف ي ال ــ ل ــ ة.

III-3. Fill in the blanks with the letters ح خ ض ط ظ ع غ ق that you hear. Add the vowels. Note to Assistant – repeat slowly the words 2-3times:

Assistant's copy

1. ــ ن ا ــ ة	contentment 'f'	1. قناعة
2. ــ ــ ر	noon time 'm'	2. ظهر
3. ــ ن ا ــ ة	Industry, manufacture 'f'	3. صناعة
4. ــ ا ي ــ	Life 'f'	4. حياة
5. ــ ب ي ــ ة	nature 'f'	5. طبيعة
6. ــ ــ ء	light 'm'	6. ضوء
7. ــ ي ر	short 'm'	7. قصير
8. ــ ي ن / ــ ي و ن	eye/eyes 'f'/'fp'	8. عين/ عُيون
9. ــ ا ــ ل	sluggish 'm'	9. خَا مِل
10. ــ ــ ي ب	strange, stranger 'm'	10 غريب

III-3.3 Fill in the blanks with the letters ح خ ض ط ظ ع غ ق that you hear. Add the vowels:

Learner's copy

contentment 'f'	1. ___ ن ا ___ ة
noon time 'm'	2. ___ ___ ر
Industry, manufacture 'f'	3. ___ ن ا ___ ة
Life 'f'	4. ___ ي ا ___
nature 'f'	5. ___ ب ي ___ ة
light 'm'	6. ___ ___ ء
short 'm'	7. ___ ___ ي ر
eye/eyes 'f'/'fp'	8. ___ ي و ن / ___ ي ن
sluggish 'm'	9. ___ ا ___ ل
strange, stranger 'm'	10. ___ ___ ي ب

38

III-4. Fill in the blanks with the letters ق غ ع ظ ط ض خ ح that you Hear:

Assistant's copy

1. أنا سعيد.	1. أنا س ـــ ي د.
2. صَبْرُهُ	2. ـــ ب ر ه
3. صديقي عربي.	3. ـــ دي ـــ ي ـــ ر ب ي.
4. هو مريض وضعيف.	4. هو مَري ـــ و ـــ ي ف.
5. الطلاب في الصف.	5. ال ـــ ل ا ب في ال ـــ ف.
6. أخي رجل طويل ونحيف.	6. أ ـــ ي رج ل ـــ و ي ل ون ـــ ي ف.
7. أنا أعمل في وزارة الإعلام.	7. أن ا أ ـــ م ل في وزارة ال إ ـــ ل ا م.
8. عندي ثلاثة أصحاب.	8. ـــ ن دي ـــ لا ـــ ة ـــ ص ـــ ب.
9. محطة القطار بعيدة.	9. م ـــ ة ال ـــ ا ر ب ـــ ي د ة.
10. هذا نبات غريب.	10. هـٰذا ن ب ا ت ـــ ري ب.

39

III- 4.4 Fill in the blanks with the letters ح خ ض ص ط ظ ع غ ق that you hear:

Learner's copy

1. أنا سـ ـــ ي د.
2. ـــ ب ر ه.
3. ـــ د ي ـــ ي ـــ ر ب ي.
4. هو مري ـــ و ـــ ـــ ي ف.
5. ال ـــ ل ـــ ا ب فِي ال ـــ ف.
6. أ ـــ ي رج ل ـــ وي ل ون ـــ ي ف.
7. أن ا أ ـــ م ل في وزَارة ال إ ـــ ل ا م.
8. ـــ ن دي ـــ لا ـــ ة ـــ ص ـــ ب.
9. م ـــ ة ال ـــ ار ب ـــ ي د ة.
10. هٰ ذا ن ب ا ت ـــ ري ب.

40

Notes:

Section IV: Connections of Letters

General Rules:

1. In Arabic, reading and writing connected or unconnected letters progress from the right side of the page to the left.

2. In writing, all Arabic letters join from both sides except for six (6) letters: (ا د ذ ر ز و) These letters join with letters preceding them or written unconnected.

3. The table below displays these letters. Practice writing to remember the shapes and comparable sounds in English:

Letters as Connected and Unconnected

Unconnected at the end of the word	Connected at the end of the word	Connected within the word	Connected at the beginning	Sound of letters	Name of Arabic letters		
ا alif maqsoora ى	ـا connected alif maqsoora ـى	ـا	none	eh ا ىٰ (aa) Alif maqsoora	alif ألِف	1	١
ب	ـب	ـبـ	بـ	b ب	baa' باء	2	٢
ت ، ة	ـت ، ـة	ـتـ	تـ	t ت	taa' تاء	3	٣
ث	ـث	ـثـ	ثـ	th ث	'thea' as in thumb* ثاء	4	٤
ـج	ـج	ـجـ	جـ	J, g ج	jeem جيم	5	٥

42

ح	ـح	ـحـ	حـ	ح*	حاء*	6 ٦
خ	ـخ	ـخـ	خـ	خ*	خاء*	7 ٧
د	ـد	ـد	د	د d	دال dal	8 ٨
ذ	ـذ	ـذ	ذ	ذ the	ذال thal	9 ٩
ر	ـر	ـر	ر	ر r	راء raa'	10 ١٠
ز	ـز	ـز	ز	ز z	زاء zaa'	11 ١١
س	ـس	ـسـ	سـ	س s	سين seen	12 ١٢
ش	ـش	ـشـ	شـ	ش sh	شين sheen	13 ١٣
ص	ـص	ـصـ	صـ	ص* sod*	صاد sod*	14 ١٤
ض	ـض	ـضـ	ضـ	ض* dhad*	ضاد dhad*	15 ١٥

43

ط	ـط	ـطـ	طـ	ط*	طاء*	16 ١٦
ظ	ـظ	ـظـ	ظـ	ظ*	ظاء*	17 ١٧
ع	ـع	ـعـ	عـ	ع*	عين*	18 ١٨
غ	ـغ	ـغـ	غـ	غ*	غين*	19 ١٩
ف	ـف	ـفـ	فـ	ف f	فاء faa'	20 ٢٠
ق	ـق	ـقـ	قـ	ق*	قاف* qaf	21 ٢١
ك	ـك	ـكـ	كـ	ك k	كاف kaf	22 ٢٢
ل	ـل	ـلـ	لـ	ل l	لام lam	23 ٢٣

						24 ٢٤
م	ـم	ـمـ	مـ	m	م meem	ميم
ن	ـن	ـنـ	نـ	n	ن noon	نون	25 ٢٥
ه	ـه	ـهـ	هـ	h	ه هـ haa'	هاء	26 ٢٦
و	ـو	ـو	و	w	و waw	واو	27 ٢٧
ي	ـي	ـيـ	يـ	y	ي yaa'	ياء	28 ٢٨
ء	ـاء ـء أ alif with hamza	ـئـ	أ	eh	أ ء Hamza	هَمْزَة	29 ٢٩
ؤ		ـؤ	none	Hamza on wow - short sound vowel damma	ؤ ou	

(*) No comparable letter or sounds in English

- **Connection of Letters**   ا د ذ ر ز و

(prince)   أَ + مِ + يْ + رـ = أَمِيْـر

(name 'm')   ه/هـ + ا + رـ + و + ن = هَـارُون

(houses 'fp')   دُ + وْ + رْ = دُوْر

(intelligent 'm')   ذَ + كِ + يّ = ذَكِيّ

(goes 'm')   يَ + ذْ + هَ + بُ = يَـذْهَـبُ

(merciful 'm')   رَ + حِ + يـ + مٌ = رَحِيمٌ

(a visit 'f')   زِ + يَ + ا + رَ + ة = زِيَـارَة

(promised)   وَ + عَ + دَ = وَعَـدَ

(hearts 'fp')   قُ + لُ + و + بْ = قُلُـوبْ

- **Ways of writing Hamza:**

Hamza (ء) is a letter. Its sound resembles the sound of alif (ا) and is primarily written on top or under (أ،إ) at the beginning of the word, within the word, or by itself at the end of the word.

Example:

1. Hamza above or under ا: (أب) father 'm' (إبْن) son 'm'
2. On Alif maqsooreh ئ: (قَارِئ) reader 'm'
3. Connected within the word as (بِــئْــر) well 'm'.) The Hamza in this form is described as sitting on a seat (كُرْسِيّ, kursi, meaning chair.) This seat allows Hamza to connect to letters on both sides.

4. The **Hamza** within the word on a seat after 'ا ، د، ذ ، ر ، ز ، و' and connected to a consonant:

standing 'm'	قَائِــم
continuous 'm'	دَائِــم
wolf 'm'	ذِئْــب
president 'm'	رَئِــيس
roaring 'm'	زَئِــير
her friends 'mp'	أصْدِقَائِها
on top of و, her friends 'mp'	أصْدِقَاؤُها
temporary 'm'	مُــؤَقت
heads 'fp'	رُؤُوْس

5. The **Hamza** is written by itself when it follows the letter (ا) as:

reading 'f'	قِراءَة
her friends 'mp'	أصْدِقَاءَها
sky 'f'	سَمَاء
prosperity 'm'	رَخَاء
air 'm'	هَوَاء

6. The **Hamza** is written at the end of the word on top of (ئ) as:

a thing 'm'   شَــيْــئ

Notes:

Test IV: Letter Writing and Letter Connection

Test IV-Section 1:

1-1. Connect the following letters. Add the vowels:

- **Greetings** التَّحِيَّة

Peace be upon you

اَلْ + سَّ + لَا + مُ   عَ + لَ + يْ + كُ + مْ =

_____

A polite response to Peace be upon you

وَ + عَ + لَ + يْ + كُ + مُ   ألْ + سَّ + لَا + مْ =

_____

Hello, Welcome

مَ + رْ + خَ + بَ + أً = _____

Good morning

صَ + بَ + ا + حُ   أل + خَ + يْ + رِ =

_____

A polite response to "Good morning"

صَ + بَ + ا + حُ   أل + نُّ + وْ + رِ =

_____

Good evening

مَ + سَ + اءُ   أل + خَ + يْ + رِ =

_____

48

A polite response to "Good evening"

مَ + سَ + ا + ءُ   أَلْ + نُّ + وْ + رْ =

How are you?

كَ + يْ + فَ   أَ لْ + حَ + ا + لْ؟ =

I am **well**, thank you.

أ + نَ + ا   بِ + خَ + يْ + رْ ، شُ + كْ + رَ + اً =

I am **good**, thank you.

أ + نَ + ا   جَ + يِّ + دْ ، شُ + كْ + رَ + اً =

I am **perfect**, thank you.

أ + ن + ا   تَ + مَ + ا + مْ ، شُ + كْ + رَ + اً =

Welcome

أ + هْـ + لَاً   وَ سَ + هْـ + لَاً = _____

See you again soon, thank you. Or, until we meet again, thank you.

إ + لَ + ى   أَلْ + لِّ + قَ + ا + ءْ ، شُ + كْ + رَ + اً =

49

- **Family members** 'mp'   أفْرَادُ ٱلْعَائِلة

Father 'm'	أ + بْ =	_____
My father	أ + بِ + يْ =	_____
Mother 'f'	أُ + مْ =	_____
My mother	أُ + مِّ + يْ =	_____
Brother 'm'	أ + خْ =	_____
My brother	أ + خِ + يْ =	_____
Sister 'f'	أُ + خْ + ت	_____
My sister	أُ + خْ + تِ + يْ =	_____
Paternal uncle 'm'	عَ + مْ =	_____
My paternal uncle	عَ + مِّ + يْ =	_____
Maternal uncle 'm'	خَ + ا + لْ =	_____
My maternal uncle	خَ + ا + لِ + يْ =	_____
Paternal aunt 'f'	عَ + مَّ + ة =	_____

My paternal aunt	عَ + مّ + تِ + يْ =	_____
Maternal aunt 'f'	خ + ا + لَ + ة =	_____
My maternal aunt	خَ + ا + لَ + تِ + يْ =	_____
Grandfather 'm'	جَ + دٌّ =	_____
My grandfather	جَ + دِّ + يْ =	_____
Grandmother 'f'	جَ + دّ + ة =	_____
My grandmother	جَ + دّ + تِ + يْ =	_____

- **In the house**   فِي البَيْت (الدَّار)

house 'm'	بَ + يْ + تْ =	_____
room 'f'	غُ + رْ + فَ + ة =	_____
window 'm'	شُ + بّ + ا + كْ =	_____
bathroom 'm'	حَ + مّ + ا + مْ =	_____
table 'f'	طَ + ا + وِ + ة =	_____
bed 'm'	سَ + رِ + يْ + رْ =	_____
chair 'm'	كُ + رْ + سِ + يْ =	_____

kitchen 'm'	مَ + طْ + بَ + خْ = _____
bedroom 'f'	غُ + رْ + فَ + ةُ ٱلْ + نَّ + وْ + مِ = _____
living room 'f'	غُ + رْ + فَ + ةُ ٱلْ + ضُّ + يْ + و + ف = _____
family room 'f'	غُ + رْ + فَ + ةُ ٱلْ + عَ + ا + ءِ + لَ + ة = _____
dining room 'f'	غُ + رْ + فَ + ةُ ٱلْ + طَّ + عَ + ا + مِ = _____

- **Clothing**   مَلابِس _ 'fp'

shoes 'fp'	أ + خْ + ذِ + يَ + ة = _____
dress 'm'	فُ + سْ + تَ + ا + نْ = _____
pants 'm'	بَ + نْ + طَ + لُ + و + نْ = _____
or	
pants 'm'	سِ + رْ + وَ + ا + لْ = _____
shirt 'm'	قَ + مِ + يْ + صْ = _____
hat 'f'	قُ + بَّ + عَ + ة = _____

jacket 'm'   جَ + ا + كَ + يْ + تْ = _____

short jacket 'f'   سُ + تْ + رَ + ة = _____

coat 'm'   مِ + عْ + طَ + ف = _____

socks 'fp'   جَ + وَ + ا + رِ + يْ + بْ = _____

bag 'f'   حَ + قِ + يْ + بَ + ة = _____

blouse 'f'   بُ + لْ + وْ + زَ + ة = _____

gown 'm'   رِ + دَ + ا + ءْ + طَ + وِ + يْ + لْ =
_____

• **Colors**   ألْوَان 'fp'

black 'm'   أ + سْ + وَ + دْ = _____

red 'm'   أ + حْ + مَ + رْ = _____

green 'm'   أ + خْ + ضَ + رْ = _____

white 'm'   أ + بْ + يَ + ضْ = _____

blue 'm'   أ + زْ + رَ + قْ = _____

black 'f'   سَ + وْ + دَ + ا + ءْ = _____

53

red 'f'   خَ + مْ + ا + رَ + ءْ = _____

green 'f'   خَ + ضْ + ا + رَ + ءْ = _____

white 'f'   بَ + يْ + ضَ + ا + ءْ = _____

blue 'f'   زَ + رْ + قَ + ا + ءْ = _____

• **Food (fruits and vegetable)**   طَعَام (فَواكِه وخُضَار)

apricots 'mp'   مِ + شْ + مِ + شْ = _____

apples 'mp'   تُ + فَّ + ا + حْ = _____

grapes 'mp'   عِ + نَ + بْ = _____

banana 'mp'   مَ + وْ + زْ = _____

peach 'mp'   خَ + وْ + خْ = _____

onions 'mp'   بَ + صَ + لْ = _____

cucumbers 'mp'   خِ + يَ + ا + رْ = _____

carrots 'mp'   جَ + زْ + رْ = _____

potatoes 'fp'   بَ + طَ + ا + طَ + ا = _____

tomatoes 'fp'   طَ + مَ + ا + طِ + مْ = _____

- **Nature**   طَـبِـيْعَـة

tree 'f'	شَ + جَ + رَ + ة = _____
trees 'fp'	أ + شْ + جَ + ا + رْ = _____
flower 'f'	وَ + رْ + دَ + ة = _____
flowers 'fp'	وُ + رُ + وْ + دْ = _____
grass 'mp'	حَ + شِ + يْ + شْ = _____
river 'm'	نَ + هْ + رْ = _____
rivers 'fp'	أ + نْ + هَ + ا + رْ = _____
sea 'm'	بَ + حْ + رْ = _____
seas 'fp'	بِ + حَ + ا + رْ = _____
mountain 'm'	جَ + بَ + لْ = _____
mountains 'fp'	جِ + بَ + ا + لْ = _____
hill 'm'	تَ + لْ = _____
hills 'fp'	تِ + لَ + ا + لْ = _____

- **Animals**   حَيَوَانَات

dog 'm'	كَ + لْ + بْ = _____
cat 'f'	قِ + طَّ + ة = _____
cow 'f'	بَ + قَ + رَ + ة = _____
sheep 'm'	خَ + رُ + وْ + فْ = _____
horse 'm'	حِ + صَ + ا + نْ = _____
donkey 'm'	حِ + مَ + ا + رْ = _____
deer 'f'	غَ + زَ + ا + لَ + ة = _____
wolf 'm'	ذِ + ءْ + بْ = _____
fox 'm'	ثَ + عْ + لَ + بْ = _____
bird 'm'	طَ + يْ + رْ = _____

- **Transportation**   مُوَاصَلَات

car 'f'	سَ + يَّ + ا + رَ + ة = _____
bus 'm'	بَ + ا + صْ = _____

bus 'f'   حَ + ا + فِ + لَ + ة = _____

bicycle 'f'   دَ + رَّ + ا + جَ + ة   هَ + وَ + ا + ءِ + يَّ + ة =

_____

motorbike 'f'   دَ + رَّ + ا + جَ + ة   غَ + ا + زِ + يَّ + ة =

_____

truck 'm'   شَ + ة + حِ + ا + نَ = _____

train 'm'   قِ + طَ + ا + رْ = _____

station 'f'   مَ + حَ + طَّ + ة = _____

airplane 'f'   طَ + ا + ءِ + رَ + ة = _____

helicopter 'f'   طَ + ا + ءِ + رَ + ة   عَ + مُ + و + دِ + يَّ + ة =

_____

airport 'm'   مَ + طَ + ا + رْ = _____

tank 'f'   دَ + بَّ + ا + بَ + ة = _____

ship 'f'   بَ + ا + خِ + رَ + ة = _____

boat 'm'   قَ + ا + رِ + بْ = _____

- **Academic level**   مُستَوىٰ الدِّراسَة

school 'f'   مَ + دْ + رَ + سَ + ة = _____

elementary 'f'   مَ + دْ + رَ + سَ + ة + اِ + بْ + تِ + ا + دَ + ا + ءِ + يَّ + ة =
_____

middle 'f'   مَ + دْ + رَ + سَ + ة + مُ + تَ + وَ + سِّ + طَ + ة =
_____

High 'f'   مَ + دْ + رَ + سَ + ة + ثَ + ا + نَ + وِ + يَّ + ة =
_____

college 'f'   كُ + لِّ + يَّ + ة = _____

university 'f'   جَ + ا + مِ + عَ + ة = _____

- **School supplies** أدَوات مَدْرَسِيَّة

pencil 'm'   ق َ + ل َ + م ْ   ر َ + ص َ + ا + ص ْ =

_____

pen 'm'   ق َ + ل َ + م ْ   ح ِ + ب ْ + ر ْ =

_____

eraser 'f'   م ِ + م ْ + ح َ + ا + ة = _____

notebook 'm'   د َ + ف ْ + ت َ + ر ْ = _____

notebooks 'fp'   د َ + ف ْ + ت ِ + ا + ر ْ = _____

paper 'f'   و َ + ر َ + ق + ة = _____

papers 'fp'   أ + و ْ + ر َ + ا + ق ْ = _____

ruler 'f'   م َ + س ْ + ط َ + ر َ + ة = _____

board 'f'   ل َ + و ْ + ح َ + ة = _____

chalks 'mp'   طَ + ب + ا + شِ + يْ + رْ = _____

computer 'm'   حَ + ا + سُ + و + بْ = _____

book 'm'   كِ + تَ + ا + بْ = _____

books 'fp'   كُ + تُ + بْ = _____

dictionary 'm'   قَ + ا + مُ + وْ + س = _____

dictionaries 'fp'   قَ + وَ + ا + مِ + ي + سْ = _____

encyclopedia 'f'   مَ + وْ + سُ + وْ + عَ + ة = _____

- **Vowels** حَرَكَات

FatHa 'f'   فَ + تْ + حَ + ة = _____

Kasra 'f'   كَ + سْ + رَ + ة = _____

Damma 'f'   ضَ + مّ + ة = _____

Sukoon 'm'   سُ + كُ + وْ + نْ = _____

Nunation 'm'   تَ + نْ + وِ + يْ + نْ = _____

Nunation of FatHa   تَ + نْ + وِ + يْ + نْ   أَلْ + فَ + تْ + حَ + ةٌ =

Nunation of Kasra   تَ + نْ + وِ + يْ + نْ   أَلْ + كَ + سْ + رَ + ةٌ =

Nunation of Damma   تَ + نْ + وِ + يْ + نْ   أَلْ + ضَّ + مّ + ةٌ =

Shadda 'f'   شَ + دّ + ةٌ = _____

Shadda _ FatHa 'f'   شَ + دّ + ةٌ   فَ + تْ + حَ + ةٌ =

Shadda _ Kasra 'f'   شَ + دّ + ةٌ   كَ + سْ + رَ + ةٌ =

Shadda _ Damma 'f'   شَ + دّ + ةٌ   ضَ + مّ + ةٌ =

Madda 'f'   مَ + دَّ + ة = _____

Wesleh 'f'   وَ + صْ + لَ + ة = _____

- **Connection of Al-Hamza**   الـهَـمْـزَة

winter 'm'   شِ + تَ + ا + ءْ = _____

airplane 'f'   طَ + ا + ئِ + رَ + ة = _____

lung 'f'   رِ + ءَ + ة = _____

chief 'm'   رَ + ئِ + يْ + سْ = _____

chief 'f'   رَ + ئِ + يْ + سَ + ة = _____

posture, look 'f'   هَـ + يْ + ءَ + ة = _____

question 'm'   سُ + ؤ + ا + لْ = _____

questions 'fp'   أ + سْ + ئِ + لَ + ة = _____

Mercury 'm'   زِ + ءْ + بَ + قْ = _____

- **Nouns**   أَسْمَاء

the telephone 'm'   ا + لْ + هَ + ا + تِ + فْ = _____

the computer 'm'   ا + لْ + حَ + ا + سُ + و + بْ = _____

the television 'm'   ا + لْ + تِّ + لْ + فَ + ا + زْ = _____

the picture 'f'   ا + لْ + صُّ + وْ + رَ + ة = _____

story 'f'   قِ + صَّ + ة = _____

Syria 'f'   سُ + وْ + رِ + يَ + ا = _____

Egypt 'f'   مِ + صْ + رْ = _____

Iraq 'm'   عِ + رَ + ا + قْ = _____

street 'm'   شَ + ا + رِ + عْ = _____

building 'f'   عِ + مَ + ا + رَ + ة = _____

building 'f'   بِ + ا + نَ + ي + ة = _____

sun 'f'   سْ + مْ + شَ = _____

moon 'm'   قَ + مَ + رْ = _____

star 'f'   نَ + جْ + مَ + ة = _____

sky 'f'   سَ + مَ + ا + ءْ = _____

coffee 'f'   قَ + هْ + وَ + ة = _____

tea 'm'   شّ + ا + يْ = _____

the Arabic language 'f'

ا + لْ + لُّ + غَ + ةُ   أْ + لْ + عَ + رَ + بِ + يَّ + ة =

_____

- **Pronouns**   ضَـمَـائِـر

I 'f-m,s'   أَ + نَ + ا = _____

we 'f-m,p'   نَ + حْ + نُ = _____

_____ = تِ + نْ + أ   you 'fs'

_____ = تَ + نْ + أ   you 'ms'

_____ = ا + مَ + تُ + نْ + أ   you 'f-m, dual'

_____ = نَّ + تُ + نْ + أ   you 'fp'

_____ = مْ + تُ + نْ + أ   you 'mp'
Or

_____ = مْ + تُ + نْ + أ   you 'f-m,p'

_____ = يَ + هِ   she 'fs'

_____ = وَ + هُ   he 'ms'

_____ = ا + مَ + هُ   they 'f-m, dual'

_____ = نَّ + هُ   they 'fp'

_____ = مْ + هُ   they 'mp'
Or

_____ = مْ + هُ   they 'f-m,p'

- <u>**Verbs**</u>   أفعَال

_____ = بْ + تُ + كْ + أ   I write 'f-m'

65

_____ = نَ + كْ + تُ + بْ   we write 'f-m,p'

_____ = تَ + كْ + تُ + بْ   you write 'm'

_____ = تَ + كْ + تُ + بِ + ي + نْ   you write 'f'

_____ = تَ + كْ + تُ + بَ + ا + نْ   you write 'f-m,dual'

_____ = تَ + كْ + تُ + بْ + نَ   you write 'fp'

_____ = تَ + كْ + تُ + بْ + و + نْ   you write 'mp'

Or

_____ = تَ + كْ + تُ + بْ + و + نْ   you write 'f-m,p'

_____ = تَ + كْ + تُ + بْ   she writes 'f'

_____ = يَ + كْ + تُ + بْ   he writes 'm'

_____ = يَ + كْ + تُ + بَ + ا + نْ   they write 'f-m,dual'

_____ = يَ + كْ + تُ + بْ + وْ + نْ   they write 'mp'

Or

_____ = يَ + كْ + تُ + بْ + وْ + نْ   they write 'f-m,p'

_____ = أَ + قْ + رَ + أ   I read 'f-m'

_____ = تَ + قْ + رَ + أ   she reads 'f'

_____ = يَ + قْ + رَ + أ   he reads 'm'

_____ = يَ + قْ + رَ + آ + نْ   they read 'f-m,dual'

_____ = يَ + قْ + رَ + أ + نَ   they read 'fp'

_____ = يَ + قْ + رَ + أُ + و + ن   they read 'f-m,p'

_____ = أ + نَ + ا + مُ   I sleep 'f-m'

_____ = تَ + نَ + ا + مُ   she sleeps 'f'

_____ = ي + نَ + ا + مُ   he sleeps 'm'

_____ = يَ + نَ + ا + مُ + وْ + نْ   they sleep 'mp'

Or

_____ = يَ + نَ + ا + مُ + وْ + نْ   they sleep 'f-m,p'

_____ = أ + أ + كُ + لْ   I eat 'f-m'

_____ = نَ + أ + كُ + لْ   we eat 'f-m,p'

_____ = تَ + أ + كُ + لِ + يْ + نْ   you eat 'f'

_____ = تَ + أ + كُ + لْ   you eat 'm'

_____ = تَ + أ + كُ + لْ + نَ   you eat 'fp'

_____ = تَ + أ + كُ + لْ + وْ + نْ   you eat 'mp'

OR

you eat 'f-m,p'   تَ + أ + كُ + وْ + نْ = _____

she eats 'f'   تَ + أ + كُ + لْ = _____

he eats 'm'   يَ + أ + كُ + لْ = _____

they eat 'mp'   يَ + أ + كُ + لُ + وْ + نْ = _____

Or

they eat 'f-m,p'   يَ + أ + كُ + لُ + وْ + نْ = _____

I run 'f-m'   أ + رْ + كُ + ضْ = _____

we run 'f-m,p'   نَ + رْ + كُ + ضْ = _____

you run 'f'   تَ + رْ + كُ + ضِ + يْ + نْ = _____

you run 'f-m,p'   تَ + رْ + كُ + ضُ + وْ + نْ = _____

you run 'fp'   تَ + رْ + كُ + ضْ + نَ = _____

- **Cardinal numbers**   أعْدادٌ

zero 'm'   • رْ + فْ + صِ = _____

68

one 'm'	١	وَ + ا + حِ + دْ = _____
one 'f'	١	وَ + ا + حِ + دَ + ة = _____
two 'm'	٢	إ + ثْ + نَ + ا + نْ = _____
two 'f'	٢	إ + ثْ + نَ + تَ + ا + نْ = _____
three 'f'	٣	ثَ + لَ + ا + ثَ + ة = _____
four 'f'	٤	أ + رْ + بَ + عَ + ة = _____
five 'f'	٥	خَ + مْ + سَ + ة = _____
six 'f'	٦	سِ + تَّ + ة = _____
seven 'f'	٧	سَ + بْ + عَ + ة = _____
eight 'f'	٨	ثَ + مَ + ا + نِ + يَ + ة = _____
nine 'f'	٩	تِ + سْ + عَ + ة = _____
ten 'f'	١٠	عَ + شْ + رَ + ة = _____
Eleven 'f'	١١	إ + حْ + دَ + ى‍ + عَ + شْ + رَ + ة + (سَ ا عَ ةً) = _____

Eleven 'm'	١١ أَ + حَ + دَ عَ + شَ + رَ + (يَومَأً) =
twelve 'f'	١٢ إِ + ثْ + نَ + تَ + ا عَ + شْ + رَ + ةَ + (سَاعَةً) =
twelve 'm'	١٢ إِ + ثْ + نَ + ا عَ + شَ + رَ + (يَومَأً) =
thirteen 'f'	١٣ ثَ + لَ + ا + ثَ عَ + شْ + رَ + ةَ + (سَاعَةً) =
thirteen 'm'	١٣ ثَ + لَ + ا + ثَ + ةَ عَ + شَ + رَ + (يَومَأً) =
fourteen 'f'	١٤ أَ + رْ + بَ + عَ عَ + شْ + رَ + ةَ + (سَاعَةً) =
fourteen 'm'	١٤ أَ + رْ + بَ + عَ + ةَ عَ + شَ + رَ + (يَومَأً) =
fifteen 'f'	١٥ خَ + مْ + سَ عَ + شْ + رَ + ةَ + (سَاعَةً) =

١٥ fifteen 'm'   خَ + مْ + سَ + ةَ   عَ + شَ + رَ + (يَ و مَ أ) = _____

- **Ordinal numbers**   أعْدادْ تَرتيبِيَّة

first 'm'	أ + لَ + وَّ + لْ =	_____
first 'f'	أُ + لَ + وْ + ى =	_____
second 'm'	ثَ + ا + نِ + يْ =	_____
second 'f'	ثَ + ا + نِ + يَ + ة =	_____
third 'm'	ثَ + ا + لِ + ثْ =	_____
third 'f'	ثَ + ا + لِ + ثَ + ة =	_____
fourth 'm'	رَ + ا + بِ + عْ =	_____
fourth 'f'	رَ + ا + بِ + عَ + ة =	_____
fifth 'm'	سْ + مِ + ا + خَ =	_____

fifth 'f'	خَ + ا + مِ + سَ + ة = _____
sixth 'm'	سَ + ا + دِ + سْ = _____
sixth 'f'	سَ + ا + دِ + سَ + ة = _____
seventh 'm'	سَ + ا + بِ + عْ = _____
seventh 'f'	سَ + ا + بِ + عَ + ة = _____
eighth 'm'	ثَ + ا + مِ + نْ = _____
eighth 'f'	ثَ + ا + مِ + نَ + ة = _____
ninth 'm'	تَ + ا + سِ + عْ = _____
ninth 'f'	تَ + ا + سِ + عَ + ة = _____
tenth 'm'	عَ + ا + شِ + رْ = _____
tenth 'f'	عَ + ا + شِ + رَ + ة = _____
eleventh 'm'	ح + ا + دِ + ي عَ + شَ + رْ =

eleventh 'f'   حَ + ا + دِ + يَ + ةَ   عَ + شْ + رَ + ة =

twelfth 'm'   ثَ + ا + نِ + يَ   عَ + شَ + رْ =

twelfth 'f'   ثَ + ا + نِ + يَ + ة   عَ + شَ + رَ + ة =

- **Days of the week**   أيَّامُ الأُسْبُوع

Saturday   ا + لْ + سَّ + بْ + تْ = _____

Sunday   ا + لْ + أَ + حَ + دْ = _____

Monday   ا + لْ + إ + ثْ + نَ + يْ + نْ =

Tuesday   ا + لْ + ثُّ + لَ + ا + ثَ + ا + ءُ =

Wednesday   ا + لْ + أَ + رْ + بِ + عَ + ا + ءُ =

_____

Thursday   ا + لْ + خَ + مِ + يْ + سْ = _____

Friday   ا + لْ + جُ + مُ + عَ + ة = _____

- **Months**   الأَشْهُـر

Arabic names

January   كَ + ا + نُ + و + نْ   ا + لْ + أ + ثَّ + ا + نِ + يْ = _____

_____

February   شُ + ب + ا + طْ = _____

March   آ + ذَ + ا + رْ = _____

April   نْ + ا + سَ + يْ + نِ = _____

May   سْ + يْ + ا + مَ = _____

74

June   حُ + رَ + يْ + ا + نْ = _____

July   تَ + مُّ + وْ + زْ = _____

August   آ + بْ = _____

September   أ + يْ + لُ + وْ + لْ = _____

October   تِ + شْ + رِ + يْ + ن   أ + لْ + أَّ + وْ + لْ = _____

November   تِ + شْ + رِ + يْ + ن   أ + لْ + ثَّ + ا + نِ + يْ = _____

December   كَ + ا + نُ + وْ + ن   أ + لْ + أ + وَّ + لْ = _____

- **Western Months in Arabic**

January   يَ + نَ + ا + يِ + رْ = _____

75

February	فَ + بْ + رَ + ا + يِ + رْ = _____
March	مَ + ا + رِ + سْ = _____
April	إِ + بْ + رِ + يْ + لْ = _____
May	مَ + ا + يُ + وْ = _____
June	يُ + وْ + نْ + يِ + وْ = _____
July	يُ + وْ + لْ + يِ + وْ = _____
August	أُ + غُ + سْ + طُ + سْ = _____
September	سَ + بْ + تَ + مْ + بْ + رْ = _____
October	أُ + كْ + تُ + وْ + بْ + رْ = _____
November	نُ + و + فَ + مْ + بْ + رْ = _____
December	دِ + ي + سَ + مْ + بْ + رْ = _____

Notes:

Test IV-Section 2:

2-1. Match each word with its correct combination of letters then write the corresponding number on the line:

١. مِفْتاحْ	___ crescent 'm' هِ + لَ + ا + لْ
٢. وَجْهْ	___ needle 'm' إِ + بْ + رَ + ة
٣. هٰذا	___ eye 'f' عَ + يْ + ن
٤. هَرَم	___ this 'f' هٰ + ذِ + ة
٥. هِلَالْ	___ pearl 'f' لُ + ؤَ + لُ + وَ + ة
٦. عَيْن	___ this 'm' هٰ + ذَ + ا
٧. إِبْرَة	___ key 'm' مِ + فْ + تَ + ا + حْ
٨. حِذَاء	___ face 'm' وَ + جْ + ه
٩. هٰذِهِ	___ pyramid 'm' هَ + رَ + م
١٠. لُؤْلُؤَة	___ shoe 'm' حِ + ذَ + ا + ء

2-2. Rewrite the following letter combinations as connected in the order that matches the word next to it. Add the correct vowels to each letter:

Lebanese 'm'   لُبْنَانِيْ   يْ + بْ + ا + لْ + نْ + نْ = _____

Sudani 'm'	سُودَانِيْ	س + و + د + ا + ن + ي + و = _____
Physician 'm'	طَبِيْب	ب + ي + ط + ب = _____
Engineer 'm'	مُهَنْدِس	م + س + ن + د + ه = _____
Egyptian 'm'	مِصْرِيْ	م + ي + ر + ص = _____
Syrian 'm'	سُوْرِيْ	س + ر + و + ي = _____
Jordanian 'm'	أُرْدُنِّي	ن + د + أ + ر + ي = _____
Iraqi 'm'	عِراقِي	ي + ر + ا + ع + ق + ي = _____
Saudi 'm'	سَعُوْدِيْ	س + ع + د + و + ي = _____
Libyan 'm'	لِيْبِيْ	ب + ي + ل + ي = _____

2-3. Write the missing letter/s in the letter combinations for the following words. Add the correct vowels:

breakfast 'm'	فُطُور	___ + و + ___ + ف + ___
my office 'm'	مَكْتَبِي	___ + ك + ___ + ___ + ي

ي + ‗ + ‗ + ب	بَيْتِي	my house 'm'
‗ + ف + ت + ‗	غُرْفَتِي	my room 'f'
‗ + ب + ت + ك	كِتَابِي	my book 'm'
‗ + ق + ‗ + ‗	صَدِيقِي	my friend 'm'
‗ + ‗ + و + م	مُوَظَّفَة	employee 'f'
‗ + ‗ + ن	نَاسْ	people 'mp'
ي + ‗ + ‗ + ‗ + خ + ‗	أَخَوَاتِي	my sisters 'fp'
ي + ‗ + و + ‗ + إ	إِخْوَتِي	my brothers 'mp'

2-4. Fill in the blanks with the missing Arabic letter/s as connected or unconnected. Add the vowels that match their transliteration in English:

س ‗ ‗	seyyed (Mr./master) 'm'
‗ د ‗ ر ‗ ـة	muderriseh (teacher) 'f'
و ‗ ‗ ر	wezeer/weziir (minister/cabinet secretary) 'm'
ه‍ـ د ‗ ‗	hedii(ee)yyeh (gift) 'f'
أُ ‗ ت ‗ ‗ ي	ustaathii/ ustaathee (my teacher/professor) 'm'
م‍ـ ز ‗	mekhzen (store) 'm'

ـــ بـــ كـــ	mektebeh (library) 'f'
ـــ ـــ ن ا ـــ	binayeh (building) 'f'
م ـــ ا ـــ س	medaris (schools) 'fp'
ك ل ـــ ـــ ت	kulliyat (colleges) 'fp'
ـــ ـــ ع ـــ ج	jami-aat (universities) 'fp'
ك ـــ ب ـــ	kutub (books) 'fp'
ـــ ب ـــ ـــ م	(melabis) 'fp'
ـــ ت ـــ ي ـــ	buyoot (houses) 'fp'
ـــ ت ـــ ـــ م	mekaatib (offices) 'fp'
ـــ د ـــ د	sudood (dams) 'fp'
ق و ب	quloob (hearts) 'fp'
ش ـــ ـــ ب ـــ ك	shebabiik/shebabeek (windows) 'fp'
ـــ ـــ ا ـــ ا ـــ	seyyarat (cars) 'fp'
ـــ ـــ و ـــ ـــ	abwab (doors) 'fp'

Notes:

Section V: Vocabulary
Reading and Memorizing

قِراءَة وَحِفْظ المُفْرَدات

In sections **I- IV,** the objective is to lead the students through steps that help them start reading. As they better recognize the forms and sounds of the letters, students will start spelling out the letters, blending each letter at a time, together with their respective vowels. They can sound letters out clearly to pronounce the whole word and be able to practice writing it in its connected letter form.

The following are straightforward steps for reading. Follow these steps to practice. Memorize the words you read.

Example: The word **book** 'm'. The Arabic separate letters for a book are:

كِ ت ا ب

Step 1- Pronounce the first letter with its vowel (كِ ، ـكِ) as 'Ki'

Step 2- Pronounce the second letter with the vowel (تَ ، ـتَـ) as 'te'

Step 3- Add the second letter to the first, separate or connected, with its vowel

(كِ ـ + تَ ، كِـتَـ) as 'ki + te'

Step 4- Pronounce the third letter (ا) as 'aa' and add it to the first and second letters (كِـ + تَ + ا ، كِـتَا) as 'ki + te + aa'

Step 5- Pronounce the three letters together (كِ ت ا ، كِـتَا) as 'kitaa'

Step 6- Pronounce the last letter (ب) as 'b' and add it to the first three to pronounce together with all the letters with their vowels: (كِ ت ا ب ، كِتَاب) as 'Kitaab.'

Repeating the pronunciation of the word helps students to master reading and writing without hesitation. Repetition is the tool that lets students memorize the word or visualize it as written.

Step 7- Follow the steps above to practice reading and writing the following words:

1. School   مَ دْ رَ سَ ة

2. Professor   أُ سْ تَ ا ذ

3. Teacher   مُ دَ رِّ س

4. College   كُ لِّ يَّ ة

5. University   جَ ا مِ عَ ة

Notes:

Test V: Vocabulary

Following the steps for reading and writing in Section V, students can practice reading the words from Section IV: **Connection of Letters** and memorize their English meanings to build their Arabic vocabulary. This vocabulary is essential for completing the following tests in Section **V** and engaging in basic conversation:

V-1. Choose the Arabic word that matches the meaning of the *underlined* word in the English sentence, then read it:

He is <u>my professor</u> at the college.   Number ❸ is a sample answer

① الْعَرَبي   ② اللُّغَةُ   ❸ أُسْتَاذِي

- The building is <u>big</u>.

① بَعِيْدَة   ② كَبِيرَة   ③ صَغِيرَة

- The <u>college</u> is far.

① طَاوِلة   ② كُلِّيَّة   ③ مَدْرَسَة

- I learned the Arabic Language in <u>Iraq</u>.

① كَنَدَا   ② عِرَاق   ③ سُوريا

- I study in the <u>evening</u>.

① بَاب   ② المَسَاء   ③ كِتَاب

- I work in the <u>morning</u>.

① الصَّبَاح   ② قَلَم   ③ سَرِيع

- My father is Egyptian.

  ① أُمّي   ② مِصْرِي   ③ أبِي

- His name is Saleem.

  ① قَصِير   ② سَامِي   ③ إسْم

- There are 14 moon letters in the Arabic alphabet.

  ① سَمَاء   ② شَمْس   ③ قَمَر

- We are fifteen students in the Arabic Language class.

  ① خَمْسَة عَشَر   ② أُخْتِي   ③ وَاحِد

- The elementary school is close to my house.

  ① بَيْت   ② إبْتِدَائِيَّة   ③ غُرْفَة

- The Empire State Building in New York City is very high.

  ① بِنَايَة   ② شَارِع   ③ مَدِيْنَة

- We have the best Arabic Language course at our university.

  ① جَامِعَة   ② صَفّ   ③ اللُّغَةُ العَرَبِيَّةُ

V-2. Fill in the blanks. Choose an adequately fitting feminine or masculine Arabic word from the word bank below to create a useful sentence or phrase with the words listed. Fill your answer choice in the blank.

واسِع wide 'm'	جَمِيلَة beautiful 'f'	أَبْيَض white 'm'	سُعُودِي Saudi 'm'
جَدِيدَة new 'f'	كِتابِي my book 'm'	صَغِيرَة small 'f'	مِصْرِيّ Egyptian 'm'
طَيِّبَة nice 'f'	كَبِيرَة big 'f'	بَعِيدَة far 'f'	أَمْرِيكِيَّة American 'f'

(dog 'm') الكَلْب ـــــــــــــــــــــــــــــــــ.

(car 'f') السَّيَّارَة ـــــــــــــــــــــــــــــــــ.

(The girl 'f') البِنْت ـــــــــــــــــــــــــــــــــ.

(The room 'f') الغُرْفَة ـــــــــــــــــــــــــــــــــ.

(This is 'm') هَـٰذا ـــــــــــــــــــــــــــــــــ.

(The university 'f') الجَامِعَة ـــــــــــــــــــــــــــــــــ.

(The college 'f') الكُلِّيَّة ـــــــــــــــــــــــــــــــــ.

(The street 'm') الشَّارِع ـــــــــــــــــــــــــــــــــ.

(My friend 'm') صَدِيْقِي ـــــــــــــــــــــــــــــــــ.

(My mother 'f') أُمّي _____.

(My friend 'f') صَدِيْقَتِي _____.

(The professor 'm') الأُسْتَاذ _____.

V-3. Read all the vocabulary words in the word bank. Select a feminine or masculine Arabic synonym (a word with a similar meaning or about the same) for each word in the list below. Fill your answer choice with vowels in the blank:

kind 'm' طَيِّب	apparel 'fp' مَلَابِس	food 'm' طَعَام	darkness 'm' ظَلَام
car 'f' سَيَّارَة	cat 'f' قِطَّة	place 'm' مَكَان	wide 'm' عَرِيْض
meal 'f' وَجْبَة	friend 'm' صَدِيق	complete 'm' كَامِل	joyful 'm' فَرْحَان

List of vocabulary words

(happy 'm') سَعِيدْ/ _____

(lunch 'm') غَدَاء / _____

(transport 'f') مُواصَلَات/ _____

(vast 'm') واسِع/ _____

(nice 'm') لَطِيْفْ/ _____

(night 'm') لَيْلْ/ _____

(dress 'fp') فُسْتَان/ _____

(fruits 'fp') فَوَاكِه/ _____

(animal 'm') حَيَوان/ _____

(intact 'm') سَلِيْم/ _____

(room 'f') غُرْفة/ _____

(companion 'm') صَاحِب/ _____

V-4. Read each Arabic vocabulary word and its meaning in English in the word bank. Select a feminine or masculine Arabic antonym (or words that means the opposite) for each word in the list below. Fill your answer choice with vowels in the blank:

beautiful 'm'	جَمِيْل	black 'm'	أسْوَد	short 'm'	قَصِيْر
heavy 'm'	ثَقِيْل	wide 'm'	واسِع	broken 'm'	مَكْسُور
sad 'm'	حَزِيْن	night-time 'm'	لَيْل	new 'm'	جَدِيْد
strong 'm'	قَوِي	small 'm'	صَغِير	empty 'm'	فَارِغ

List of vocabulary words

سَلِيْم _____ (intact 'm')

خَفِيْف _____ (light 'm')

فَرْحَان _____ (happy 'm')

نَهَار _____ (day-time 'm')

(ugly 'm')	قَبِيح	_____
(old 'm')	قَدِيم	_____
(big 'm')	كَبِير	_____
(narrow 'm')	ضَيِّق	_____
(white 'm')	أَبْيَض	_____
(weak 'm')	ضَعِيف	_____
(long 'm')	طَوِيل	_____
(full 'm')	مَمْلُوء	_____

Notes:

Section VI: Interrogatives and Prepositions
الإستِفْهام والجَر

List of commonly used interrogatives and prepositions:

هَلْ؟	Is it? Do you? Did you? Will you? Is he? Is she? Is this? Is that? The answer should be either "Yes" نَعَم or "No" لَا
مَنْ؟	*Who?* (A question about a human.)
مَنْ هُوَ؟	*Who* is he?
مَنْ هِيَ؟	*Who* is she?
لِمَنْ؟	لِ *To/for whom does it belong?* (لِ *to/for/belong to,* prefixed interrogative article مَن *whom.*)
لِمَن هٰذا؟	*To/ for whom, does this belong?* 'm'
لِمَن هٰذِهِ؟	*To whom does this belong?* 'f'
مَعَ مَن؟	*With whom?* (Preposition article مَعَ *with,* مَنْ *whom.*)
مَا؟	*What?* (A question about a non-human.)
مَا هٰذا؟	*What is this?* 'm'
مَا هٰذِهِ؟	*What is this?* 'f'
مَاذا؟	*What?* (A question about an action.)
بِمَاذا؟	*With what?* (بِ *with/by* prefixed preposition article مَاذا *what.* A question addressed to a human as to ask: *with what* do you write?)

لِمَاذَا؟	ـِل Why/ for what? (ـِل for, **prefixed article** مَاذَا what. A question addressed to a human to inquire about a reason or a cause to say: *for what* are you here?)
أَيْنَ؟	Where? (A question about a place.)
مِن أَيْنَ؟	From where? (مِن from, أَيْنَ where.)
إِلَىٰ	To
إِلَىٰ أَيْنَ؟	To where? (إِلَىٰ to, أَيْنَ where.)
كَيْفَ؟	How? (A question about a condition.)
مَتَىٰ؟	When? (A question about time.)
أَي؟	Which? (A question about preference.)
كَم؟	How many? (A question about quantity.)
بِكَم؟	How much? (A question about price.)

Section VI-1
Usage samples of Interrogatives and Prepositions
Interrogatives and Prepositions for questions and possible answers:

- **هَلْ؟** *(Is it? Do you? Did you? Will you? Is he? Is she? Is this? Is that?)*

    The answer usually is *yes* **نَعَم** or *no* **لا**

Are you a student?	هَلْ أنْتَ طَالِب؟
Yes, I am a student.	نَعَم أنَا طَالِب.
Is she an Arab?	هَلْ هِيَ عَرَبِيَّة؟
No, she is American.	لَا هِيَ أمْرِيكِيَّة.

- **مَنْ؟** *(Who?)*

Who is he?	مَنْ هُوَ؟
He is my friend Ahmad.	هُوَ صَدِيقِي أحْمَد
Who is she?	مَنْ هِيَ؟
She is a professor of the Arabic language.	هِيَ أُسْتَاذَةُ اللُّغَةِ العَرَبِيَّة.

- **لِمَنْ؟** *(To/for whom?)*

For whom is this book?	لِمَنْ هَـذا الكِتَاب؟
This book is for my brother Saleem.	هَـذا الكِتَاب لِأخِي سَلِيم.
To whom does this watch belong?	لِمَنْ هَـذِهِ السَّاعَة؟
This watch belongs to my sister Mona.	هَـذِهِ السَّاعَة لِأُخْتِي مُنَى.
For whom is this food?	لِمَنْ هَـذا الطَّعَام؟
This food is for the poor.	هَـذا الطَّعَام لِلْفُقَرَاء. (The poor People)

- **مَعَ مَنْ؟** (With whom?)

With whom do you study the Arabic Language?	مَعَ مَنْ تَدرُس اللُّغَةَ العَرَبِيَّةَ؟
I study with my friend Ahmad.	أدرُسْ مع صَديقي أحْمَد.
With whom do you eat in the cafeteria?	مَعَ مَنْ تَأكُلين فِي الكَافِيتِيرِيَا؟
I eat with my friend Layla.	أأكُل (آكُل) مَعَ صديقَتي لَيْلَىٰ.

- **مَا؟** (What?)

What is your name?	مَا إسْمُكَ؟
My name is Saleem.	إسْمي سَليم.
What is your name?	مَا إسْمُكِ؟
My name is Layla.	إسْمي لَيْلَىٰ.
What is this? 'm'	مَا هٰذا؟
This is a pencil.	هٰذا قَلَم.
What are these? 'f'	مَا هٰذِهِ؟
These are Arabic books	هٰذِهِ كُتُب عَرَبِيَّة.

- **مَاذَا؟** (What do you do, what are you doing?)

What are you writing?	مَاذَا تَكْتُبْ؟
I am writing the homework.	أكْتُب الوَاجِب.
What do you eat?	مَاذَا تَأكُل؟
I eat chicken.	أأكُل (آكُل) دَجَاج.

- **بِمَاذَا؟** (With what do you ....?)

With what do you write?	بِمَاذَا أَنْتَ تَكْتُبُ؟
I write with a pencil.	أَنَا أَكْتُبُ بِالقَلَمِ.
With what do you eat?	بِمَاذَا أَنْتَ تَأْكُلُ؟
I eat with the spoon.	أنا أَأْكُل (آكُل) بِالْمِلْعَقَة.

- **لِمَاذَا؟** (Why/for what?)

Why (for what) are you sleeping لِمَاذَا أَنْتَ نَائِمٌ؟

I am sleeping because I am tired. أَنَا نَائِمٌ لِأَنِّي تَعْبَان.

Why (for what) do you study the Arabic Language?

لِمَاذَا تَدْرُسُ اللُّغَةَ العَرَبِيَّةَ؟

I study the Arabic Language to speak (or to talk لِأَتَكَلَّم) with my Arab friends.

أَنَا أَدْرُسُ اللُّغَةَ العَرَبِيَّةَ لِأَتَكَلَّم مَعَ أَصْدِقَائِي العَرَب.

- **أَيْنَ؟** (Where is/are...?)

Where is the book?	أَيْنَ الكِتَاب؟
The book is in the library.	الكِتَاب فِي المَكْتَبَة.
Where is he?	أَيْنَ هُوَ؟
He is in the classroom.	هُوَ فِي الصَّف.
Where are the students?	أَيْنَ الطُّلَّابُ؟

الطُّلَّاب فِي الجَامِعَة.	The students are in the university.
أَيْنَ البِنْت؟	*Where* is the girl?
البِنْت فِي المَدْرَسة.	The girl is in school.

• إِلــىٰ أَيْنَ؟ (Where to?)

إِلــىٰ أَيْنَ تَسِير فِي هٰذا الشَّارِع؟	*Where* are you <u>walking</u> to in this street?
أَسِيرُ فِي هٰذا الشَّارِع إِلــىٰ بَيْتِي.	I walk (أَسِيرْ) in this street (الشَّارِع) to my house.
إِلــىٰ أَيْنَ تَذهَب هٰذا المَسَاء؟	*Where* do you go to this evening?
أَذهَب هٰذا المَسَاء إِلــىٰ السِّينِمَا.	I go this evening to the movies.

• مِن أَيْنَ؟ (From where?)

مِن أَيْنَ هٰذا الكِتَاب؟	*From where* this book?
هٰذا الكِتَاب مِنْ المَكْتَبَة.	This book is from the library.
مِنْ أَيْنَ أَذْهَب إِلــىٰ الكُلِّيَّة؟	*From where* do I go to college?
تَذهَب إِلىٰ الكُلِّيَّة مِن هٰذا الشَّارِع.	You go to college from this street.

• كَيْفَ؟ (How?)

كَيْفَ حَالُكَ؟	*How* are you? 'm'
أنا بِخَير وَ شُكْراً.	I am well, thank you.
كَيْفَ حَالُكِ؟	*How* are you? 'f'
أنا بِخَير وشُكْراً.	I am well, thank you.
كَيْفَ الجَوّ /الطَّقْس اليوم؟	*How* is the weather (الجَوّ/الطَّقْس) today?

الجَوّ بَارِدٌ اليَومَ.	The weather is cold today.
كَيْفَ أنتَ الآنَ؟	*How* are you now?
أنا سَعِيْد الآنَ.	I am happy (سَعِيْد) now.
أنا تَمَام الآنَ.	I am O.K. (تَمَام) now.

- مَتــىٰ؟ (*When?*)

مَتــىٰ تَذْهَب إلىٰ المَدرَسة؟	*When* do you go to school?
أذْهَب إلىٰ المَدْرَسَة في الصَّباح.	I go to school in the morning.
مَتــىٰ دَرَسْتَ الكِيمْيَاء؟	*When* did you study Chemistry?
دَرَسْتُ الكِيمْيَاء في فَصْلِ الرَّبِيع الدِّرَاسِيّ.	I studied Chemistry in the Spring Semester.

- أَيّ؟ (*Which?* or في أَيّ *in which?* or مِنْ أَيّ *from which?*)

أَيّ طَالِبٍ نَجَحَ في الإمْتِحَان؟	*Which* student passed the exam?
أنا يا أُسْتَاذَة.	I am professor 'f'.
في أَيّ كُلِّيةٍ تَدْرُس يا أَحْمَد؟	Oh, Ahmed, *in which* college do you study?
أنا أَدْرُس في كُلِّية المَدِينَة.	I study in the City College.
مِنْ أَيّ وِلَايَةٍ أنْتَ؟	*From which* state are you?
أنا مِن وِلَايَةِ فلُورِيدَا.	I am from the state of Florida.

- (كَمْ؟ *How much* بِكَمْ؟ *how man* كَمْ/بِكَمْ؟)

كَمْ عَدَدُ الغُرَفِ في هٰذا البَيت؟	*How many* rooms are in this house?
غُرْفَةٌ وَاحِدَة في هٰذا البَيْت.	One room is in this house.

How much are the apples?
These apples are two dollars.

بِكَمْ هٰذا التُّفّاح؟
هٰذا التُّفّاح بِدولارَين.

Section VI-2
Interrogatives and Prepositions for Greeting Vocabulary:

How? كَيفَ؟	Who? مَن؟	What? مَا؟	Is it or do you? هَل؟	Where? أينَ؟
To where? إلىٰ أينَ؟	From where? مِن أينَ؟	For what? لِماذا؟	From which? مِن أيّ؟	In which? في أيّ؟
I أنا We 'm-f,p' نَحن	You 'ms' أنتَ You 'fs' أنتِ	You 'm-f,p' أنتم	He هو She هي	They 'm-f,p' هُم
Peace be with you السَّلامُ عَلَيكُم **respond:** And with you the peace وعَلَيكُم السَّلام	Good morning صَباح الخَير **respond:** صَباح النُّور	Good evening مَساء الخَير **respond:** مَساء النُّور	How is it with you? كَيف الحَال؟ **respond:** Thank God, الحَمْدُ لله Well بِخَير Perfect تَمَام	Thank you شُكراً **respond:** You're welcome عَفواً
How are you? 'm' كَيف حَالُكَ؟ **respond:** Thank God الحَمْدُ لله I am well. أنا بِخَير I am good. أنا جَيِّد. I am perfect. أنا تَمام.	How are you? 'f' كَيف حَالُكِ؟ **respond:** Thank God الحَمْدُ لله I am well. أنا بِخَير I am good. أنا جَيِّدة. I am perfect. أنا تَمام.	How are you? 'm-f,p' كَيف حَالُكُم؟ **respond:** m-f,p' We thank God. الحَمْدُ لله We are well/perfect. نحن بِخَير./نحن تمام. We are good. نَحنُ جَيِّدون.	How is he? 'm' كَيف حَالُه؟ **respond:** He, thank God. هو ، الحَمْدُ لله He is well/perfect. هو بِخَير./هو تمام. He is good. هو جَيِّد.	How is she? 'f' كَيف حَالُها؟ **respond:** She, thank God. هي ، الحَمْدُ لله She is well/perfect. هي بِخَير/هي تمام She is good. هي جَيِّدة

How are they? 'm-f,p' كَيفَ حَالُـهُم؟ **respond:** They, thank God هم ، الحَمْدُ لله They, are good. هم ، جَيِّدون They, are well. هم، بِخَيْر perfect. هم ، تَمَام	Welcome مَرحَباً General greetings for receiving guests, students in a classroom, passing friends !!	You are welcome 'm.' مَرحَباً بِكَ **respond:** Welcome, thank you مَرحَباً و شُكْراً	You are welcome 'f' مَرحَباً بِكِ **respond:** Welcome, thank you مَرحَباً و شُكْراً	You are all welcome 'm-f,p' مَرحَباً بِـكُم **respond:** Welcome, thank you مَرحَباً وشُكْراً
Welcome General greetings for receiving guests, students in a classroom أهلاً وَسَهْلاً	Welcome 'm' أهلاً وَسَهْلاً **respond for:** أهلاً وَسَهْلاً بِكَ	Welcome 'f' أهلاً وَسَهْلاً **respond:** أهلاً وَسَهْلاً بِكِ	Welcome 'm-f,p' أهلاً وَسَهْلاً **respond for:** أهلاً وَسَهْلاً بِـكُم	We are honored by you 'm-f,p' تَشَرَّفنا بِـكُم **respond:** we are, also ونحن أيضاً
Please come in تَفَضَّلوا **respond:** thank you شُكْراً	Until we meet again إلى اللِّقاء **respond:** إلى اللِّقاء	Good-by General greetings for one person or groups مَعَ السَّلامَة	May you be safe مَعَ السَّلامة **respond:** مَعَ السَّلامَة	When do we see you? 'm-f,p' مَتـى : نَراكَ/نَراكِ/ نَراكُم؟ **respond:** very soon قَريباً جِدّاً (إنْ شاء الله)

Notes:

Test VI: Conversation dialogues

VI-1. Read the Arabic vocabulary words in the word bank. Some of these words are selections of greeting answers next to each picture. Circle your answer of the word or phrase that best fits the blank bubbles in the following 1-7 dialogue scenes:

Vocabulary 1-1

وَعَلَيْكُم السَّلام	مرحباً	مَدْرَسَة	السَّلام عليكم
إسْمِي سَمِير	مَعي	أهْلاً	ما إسْمُكَ؟
سَهْلاً	أنا نُورا	سَعيد	مَنْ أنتِ؟
أنا مِن تُونِس	نَعَم	نَهار	مِنْ أيْنَ أنْتِ؟

Dialogue 1-1

Vocabulary 1-2

هَلْ أنْتِ طَالِبَة؟	إسمي	نعم أنا طَالِبَة	لَيْلَى
ماذا تَدْرُسِيْن؟	صَبَاح الخَيْر	الـلُّغَة العَرَبِيَّة	سَلَام
أيْنَ تَدْرُسِيْن ؟	شا رع	بَيْت	فِي كُلِّيَّة
ما اسْمُ الْكُلِّيَّة؟	سَمِيرَة	كُلِّيَّة الـلُّغَات	صَفُّ

Dialogue 1-2

Vocabulary 1-3

أسْتَاذ	مرحَباً بِكِ	لِمَاذا	مَرْحَباً يَا سمير
أنا بِـخَيْر شُكْراً	مُدَرِّس	مَدْرَسَة	كَيْفَ حَالُكَ؟
أنتُم	أنا أيْضاً	أهْلاً وَسَهْلاً	وأنْتَ؟
إلَى اللِّقَاءْ	مَكْتَبَة	آسِف	مَعَ السَّلَامَة

Dialogue 1-3

١

مَدْرَسَة
أسْتَاذ
مَرْحَباً بِكِ

٢

مَدْرَسَة
مُدَرِّس
أنا بِخَيْر شُكْراً

٣

اهْلاً وسَهْلاً
أنا أيْضاً بِخَيْر
أنتُم

٤

آسِف
مَكتَبَة
إلَى اللِّقَاءْ

Vocabulary 1-4

لِمَاذا	أَهْلاً وسَهْلاً	شُكْرًا	أَنا مَرْيَم
مَن أَنْتَ؟	سَلَام	تَشَرَّفنَا	يا سمير
سعيد	لا أنا أمْرِيكِيَّة	وِلَايَة	هل أنتِ عربية؟
مِن وِلَايَة تَكْسَاس	صَفّ	قَرْيَة	مِن أيْ وِلَايَة؟

Dialogue 1-4

Vocabulary 1-5

آسِف	نَعَم الحَمْدُ لِلّه	كَبِير	مَدِينَة شِيكَاغُو
فِي بَيْت	مَن أنْتَ	جَيّد	أيْنَ تَسْكُنْ؟
صَغِير	مَعَ وَالِدِي وَوَالِدَتِي	أسْتَاذ	مَعَ مَنْ تَسْكُنْ؟
شَارِع	يا سَمِير هَلْ أنْتَ بِخَيْر؟	بَلَد country	فِي أيْ مَدِينَة؟

Dialogue 1-5

مَن أنْتَ؟

نَعَم الحَمْدُ لِلّه

آسِف

جَيّد

كَبِير

فِي بَيْت

أسْتَاذ

صَغِير

مَعَ وَالِدِي وَوَالِدَتِي

مِنْطَقة

مَدِينَة شِيكَاغُو

شَارِع

Vocabulary 1-6

نَعَمْ	صَبَاح الخَيْر	مَدْرَسَة	هل تَدْرُسِيْن في الكُلِّيَّة اليَوْم؟
مُمْتَاز	في المَكْتَبَة	شُكْراً	نَعَمْ وَاجِبَات كَثِيْرَة
سَلَام	أيْنَ تَدْرُسِيْن؟	أهْلاً	هَلْ عِنْدَكِ وَاجِبَات؟
جَيِّدَة	آسِفَة عندي إخْتِبار quiz	قَهْوَة	هَلْ تَشْرَبِيْن الشَّاي مَعِي؟

Dialogue 1-6

١

نَعَم

صَبَاح الخَيْر

إسمي

٢

شُكْراً

في المَكْتَبَة

مُمْتَاز

٣

أهْلاً

سَلَام

نَعَمْ وَاجِبَات كَثِيْرَة

٤

قَهْوَة

آسِفَة عندي إخْتِبار

جَيِّدَة

Vocabulary 1-7

مَدِينَة	صَبَاح النُّور	أيْضاً	صباح الخير يا نورا
شُكْراً	عِنْدِي إمْتِحَان	كِتَاب	لِمَاذَا أنتِ فِي الكُلِّيَّة اليوم؟
وَاجِب	أيْ إمتِحان؟	مَكْتَب	الإمْتِحَان النِّهَائِي
لَا سَهْلْ	مَكْتَب	مَعَ مَنْ	هَلْ الإمتِحَان صَعب؟

Dialogue 1-7

١

أيْضاً

صَبَاحُ النُّور

مَدِينَة

٢

كِتَاب

شُكْراً

عِنْدِي إمْتِحَان

٣

أيْضاً

الإمْتِحَان النِّهَائِي

واجِب

٤

مَعَ مَنْ

مَدِينَة

لَا سَهْلْ

VI-2. Translate into Arabic the following interrogative questions and answers:

- Is he from Lebanon? No, he is from Iraq.

- When are you going to Egypt? I am going in the summer.

- How much is this book? This book is 5 dollars.

- Where is your family? My family is in Syria.

- How is your father doing? My father is doing well.

- Why do you study Arabic? Because I like the Arabic Language.

- Which language do you like? I like the American English Language.

- Why do you study medicine? Because I want to be (أن أكون) a doctor.

- Who is that American Lady? She is my teacher.

- What do you read in Arabic, now? I read a story.

VI-3. Practice with other learners reading the telephone conversation in each picture between Saleem and Samira.

Saleem (سَليم) speaks on the telephone from his hotel room. Samira (سَميرَة) answers.

VI-4. Translate the text of the telephone conversation:

سَليم ـ ألو مَنْ أنتِ؟

سَميرة ـ أنا سَميرة.

سَليم ـ هل هـٰذا بَيت الوَالِد أحمَد؟

سَميرة ـ نَعَم هـٰذا بيت الوَالِد أحْمَد.

سَليم ـ وَمَن أنتِ؟

سَميرة ـ أَنا ابنَتُهُ سَميرة.

سَليم ـ كَيفَ حَالُكِ؟

سَميرة ـ أنا بِخَير وَشُكْراً.

سَليم ـ هَل والِدُكِ في البَيت؟

سَميرة ـ لا هو في بيت عَمّي.

سَليم ـ لِماذا ذَهَبَ إلىٰ بَيتِ عَمِّكِ؟

سَميرة ـ لأنَّ عَمّي مَريض.

سَليم ــ مَتى ذَهَبَ والِدُكِ إلىٰ بَيْتِ عَمِّكِ؟

سَميرة ــ ذَهَبَ إلىٰ بيتِ عَمّي قَبْلَ ٣ سَاعات.

سَليم ــ مَتىٰ يَعُودُ إلىٰ البَيتِ؟

سَميرة ــ يَعودُ بَعْدَ سَاعَة.

سَليم ــ مِن فَضْلِكِ، سَلِّمي علىٰ والِدِكِ. إنشاء الله أُكَلِّمُه مَرةً أُخْرىٰ.

سَميرة ــ مَعَ السَّلامَة

سَليم ــ إلىٰ اللِّقاء

VI-5. In your own words, write a few lines in Arabic that summarize the telephone conversation.

VI-6. Choose the interrogative from Table 1 that best fits in the blank for each question in Column 1 of Table 2. Answers to the questions are in Column 2:

Table 1: Interrogatives

كَم	أيّ	لِماذا	مَتَىٰ	هَل
مَاذا	مَن	كَيْفَ	إِلَىٰ أَيْنَ؟	مَا

Table 2: Fill in the blanks with interrogatives

2	1
أنا أَدْرُس اللُّغَة العَرَبِيَّة.	_____ تَدْرُس في الكُلِّية؟
هٰذه كُتُبُ اللُّغَةِ الإنْجِليزِيَّة.	_____ هٰذه؟
نَعَم أكتُب الواجِب.	_____ تَكتُب الواجِب؟
سَالي ذَهَبَت إِلَىٰ مَدرَسةِ المُوسِيقَىٰ.	_____ ذَهَبَت سَالي؟
أكتُب الرِّسَالة الآن.	_____ تَكتُب الرِّسَالة؟
هُوَ صَدِيقِي أحمد.	_____ هُوَ؟

115

_____ مُوَظَفاً* مَعَكَ في المَكْتَب؟ *an employee	مُوَظَفٌ* واحِد مَعِي في المَكْتَب.
_____ لُغَةٍ تُحِب؟	أُحِبُّ اللُّغَة الفِرَنْسِيَّة.
_____ حَالُ العَائِلة؟	العَائِلَة بِخَيْر وَشُكْراً.
_____ تَشْرَبِين المَاء؟	أشْرَب المَاء لأنّي عَطْشَانَة thirsty

Notes

Section VII: Noun and Pronoun

Noun	الإسْم
Singular noun	الإسْم المُفْرَد
Plural noun	جَمْع الإسْم
Pronoun	الضَّمِير

The Noun الإسْم

- A noun is a word that refers to a person, place, animal, plant, thing, or idea.
- Except for articles, every Arabic Noun (including demonstrative nouns) is gendered.
- Nouns are either singular or plural masculine or singular or plural feminine.
- A noun is masculine and refers to an entity that is a human male such as a man رَجُل، a brother أَخ، a father أَب. A noun is feminine if it relates to a human female such as a mother أُمْ or sister أُخت.
- A noun is masculine refers to non-human entities such as train قِطَار، one وَاحِدْ. Or, feminine non-human entities ending with (ة ، ـة ، ت) as cat قِطَّة، or tree شَجَرَة، or busses حَافِلات.
- Some country names are feminine, while others are masculine.

Example:

لِيْبْيَا Libya (f)	سُورْيَا Syria (f)	الجَزائِر Algeria (f)	مِصْر Egypt (f)
السُّودان Sudan (m)	لُبْنَان Lebanon (m)	المَغْرِب Morocco (m)	العِرَاق Iraq (m)

Memorizing the feminine and masculine of Arabic nouns facilitates recognition of the grammatical position of the noun and its function in a sentence.

The singular noun الإسْم المُفْرَد is summarized in the following categories:

1. **Singular Proper Noun** إسْم خاصّ Feminine 'f' or masculine 'm', such as the specific names of people, countries, or trademarks:

    Example:

    تُويُوتا 'f' Toyota   أمريكا 'f' America   سَامْيَة Samia   أحْمَد Ahmed

    حَاسُوب Computer 'm'

2. **Singular Common Noun** إسْم عامّ Feminine 'f' or masculine 'm', as a space, an object, an idea, or abstract:

    Example:

    بَيْت house 'ms'   مَدْرَسَة school 'fs'   كِتَاب book 'ms'
    شَارِع street 'ms'   مِفْتَاح key 'ms'   غُرْفَة room 'fs'
    حَفْلَة party 'fs'   شُغْل work 'ms'   نَجَاح success 'ms'
    دَعْوَة invitation 'fs' فِكْرَة idea 'fs'   طَبِيعَة nature 'fs'

The plural noun جَمْع الإسْم references a quantity of three or more masculine and/or feminine entities. When the noun converts into a plural, it may retain part of its singular structure but change into an irregular plural form by adding or eliminating letters. At this elementary level of learning, students may have to memorize the irregular masculine and feminine plurals.

The following are examples of converting the singular noun into irregular masculine plurals, and the singular noun into feminine regular or irregular plurals. More of these examples are in Tables 1 and 2, Columns 3 and 4:

- When converting masculine المُذَكَّر human singular noun to its plural forms, it becomes irregular (broken تَكْسِير) masculine plural noun -

    رَجُل ← رِجَال (man/men) as جَمْع تَكْسِير المُذَكَّر.

- When converting masculine non-human singular noun it becomes irregular (broken تَكْسِير) feminine plural noun as (book/books) كِتَاب ← كُتُب.

118

- When converting feminine (المُؤَنَّث) human singular noun it becomes regular (sound سَالِم) feminine plural noun as جَمْع المُؤَنَّث السَّالِم (girl /girls) بِنْت ← بَنَات.

- When converting feminine non-human singular noun it becomes irregular feminine (broken تَكْسِير) plural جَمْع تَكْسِير المُؤَنَّث such as (room/rooms) غُرْفَة ← غُرَف.

Examples:

Table 1- The <u>masculine</u> irregular (broken تَكْسِير) plural noun 'mbp'

1 Masculine singular/plural	2 <u>Masculine</u> singular	3 <u>Masculine</u> broken plural	4 <u>Masculine</u> non-human broken plural
answer /answers	جَوَاب		أجْوِبَة
art/arts	فَن		فُنُون
bird/birds	طَيْر		طُيُور
book /books	كِتاب		كُتُب
boy /boys	وَلَد	أوْلاد	
center/centers	مَرْكَز		مَرَاكِز
chair/chairs	كُرْسِي		كَرَاسِي
classroom/ classrooms	صَفّ		صُفُوف

English	Singular		Plural
country/countries	بَلَد		بِلاد
cousin/maternal	إبْنُ خَال	أبْنَاءُ خَال	
cousin/paternal	إبْنُ عَم	أبْنَاءُ عَم	
department/departments	قِسْم		أقْسَام
dog/dogs	كَلْب		كِلَاب
dream/dreams	حِلْم		أحْلَام
face/faces	وَجْه		وُجُوه
factory/factories	مَصْنَع		مَصَانِع
floor/floors	طَابِق		طَوَابِق
head/heads	رَأس		رُؤُوس
heart/hearts	قَلْب		قُلُوب
hill/hills	تَل		تِلَال
homeland/homelands	وَطَن		أوْطَان
house/houses	بَيْت		بُيُوت
king/kings	مَلِك	مُلُوك	
law/laws	قَانُون		قَوَانِين
man/men	رَجُل	رِجَال	
mansion/mansions	قَصْر		قُصُور

English	Singular		Plural
moon/moons	قَمَر		أَقْمَار
mountain/mountains	جَبَل		جِبَال
museum/museums	مَتْحَف		مَتَاحِف
name/names	إسْم		أسْمَاء
news/news	خَبَر		أخْبَار
office/offices	مَكْتَب		مَكاتِب
pencil/pencils	قَلَم		أقْلام
president/presidents	رَئِيس	رُؤَسَاء	
prince/princes	أمِير	أمَراء	
restaurant/restaurants	مَطْعَم		مَطَاعِم
road/roads	طَرِيق		طُرُق
sea/seas	بَحْر		بِحَار
store/stores	مَخْزَن		مَخَازِن
street/streets	شَارِع		شَوارِع
time/times	وَقْت		أوْقَات
window/windows	شُبَّاك		شَبَابِيْك

Table 2- The <u>feminine</u> regular (sound سَالِم) plural noun 'fsp' and the irregular feminine non-human (broken تَكْسِير) plural noun 'fbp'

1 Feminine singular/plural	2 Feminine singular	3 <u>Feminine</u> regular plural	4 <u>Feminine</u> non-human broken plural
adjective/adjectives	صِفَة	صِفَات	
advisor/advisors	مُرشِدَة	مُرشِدَات	
airplane/ airplanes	طَائِرَة	طَائِرَات	
apartment/apartments	شُقَّة		شُقَق
bag/bags	حَقيبَة		حَقَائِب
building/buildings	بِنَايَة	بِنَايَات	
bus/buses	حَافِلَة	حَافِلَات	
café/cafés	مَقْهَى		مَقَاهِي
car/cars	سَيَّارَة	سَيَّارَات	
cat/cats	قِطَّة		قِطَط
chain/chains	سِلْسِلَة		سَلَاسِيل
chimney	مَدْخَنَة		مَدَاخِن
college/colleges	كُلِّيَّة	كُلِّيَّات	

computer 'm,f'	كُومْبْيوتَر ، حَاسُوب	كُومْبْيوتَرات	حَوَاسِيب
dress/dresses	فُسْتَان		فَسَاتِين
ear/ears	أُذُن		آذان
eye/eyes	عَيْن		عُيُون
fish/fish	سَمَكة		أَسْمَاك
flower/flowers	وَرْدَة		وُرُود
garden/gardens	حَدِيْقَة		حَدَائِق
girl/girls	بِنْت	بَنَات	
hospital/hospitals	مُسْتَشْفَى	مُسْتَشْفَيَات	
journal/journals/newspaper/newspapers	صَحِيفَة، جَرِيدَة		صُحُف، جَرَائِد
knife/knives	سِكِّينَة		سَكَاكِين
lake/lakes	بُحَيْرَة	بُحَيْرَات	
language/languages	لُغَة	لُغَات	
letter/letters	رِسَالَة		رَسَائِل

English	Singular	Sound Plural	Broken Plural
library/libraries	مَكْتَبة	مَكْتَبَات	
meal/meals	وَجْبة	وَجَبَات	
minute/minutes	دَقِيقة		دَقَائِق
mirror/mirrors	مِرْآة		مَرَايا
neck/necks	رَقَبة		رِقَاب
page/pages	صَفْحة	صَفَحَات	
paper/papers	وَرَقة		أَوْرَاق
picture/pictures	صُورة		صُوَر
president/presidents	رَئِيسة	رَئِيسَات	
princess/princesses	أَمِيرة	أَمِيرَات	
room/rooms	غُرْفة		غُرَف
rose/roses	زَهْرة		زُهُور، أَزْهَار
school/schools	مَدْرَسة		مَدَارِس
ship/ships	بَاخِرة		بَوَاخِر
sky/skies	سَمَاء	سَمَاوَات	

English	Singular	Plural (sound)	Plural (broken)
spoon/spoons	مِلْعَقة		مَلَاعِق
star/stars	نَجْمَة		نُجُوْم
state/states	وِلَايَة	وِلايَات	
table/tables	طَاوِلَة	طَاوِلات	
theater/theaters	مَلْهَى		مَلَاهِي
tree/trees	شَجَرَة		أشْجَار
university/universities	جَامِعَة	جَامِعَات	
watch/watches	سَاعَة	سَاعَات	
widow/widows	أرْمَلَة		أرَامِل
wife/wives	زَوْجَة	زَوْجَات	
window/windows	نَافِذَة		نَوَافِذ
woman /women	إمْرَأة		نِساء
woman /women	إمْرَأة		نِسْوَة
word/words	كَلِمَة	كَلِمَات	
year/years	سَنَة	سَنَوَات	

The Pronoun   الضَّمِيْر

The pronoun is a word that replaces the noun, and its function is similar grammatically to a noun. Like the noun, all pronouns are gendered. In Arabic, there are no gender-neutral pronouns like in English "it", for example.

The following are the basic three pronoun categories:

- **Independent personal pronoun**   ضَمِيْرٌ مُنْفَصِلْ

    1. Singular personal pronoun 'sp'   المُفْرَدْ

    Example:

English	Pronoun Form	Singular/مُفْرَد
I	1st person 'm-f,s'	أَنَا
you	2nd person 'ms'	أَنْتَ
you	2nd person 'fs'	أَنْتِ
he	3rd person 'ms'	هُوَ
she	3rd person 'fs'	هِيَ

    2. Dual unattached personal pronoun 'm-f,dp'   المُثَنَّىْ

In Arabic grammar, there is a separate form of plural pronoun that references groups of only **two** people or entities <u>called the dual plural المُثَنَّى.</u>

<u>**Note: The dual plural is not explored further nor included in Arabic 101 tests. The following table is a brief introduction to the students.**</u>

The dual pronoun المُثَنَّى *

English	Singular/مُفْرَد	Dual/مُثَنَّى
we (1st person)	أنَا	نَحْنُ
you (2nd person)	أنتَ، أنتِ	أنتُمَا
they (3rd person)	هُوَ ، هِيَ	هُمَا

(*) Masculine and feminine plural for two

3. Plural personal pronoun الجَمْعْ

The personal plural pronoun refers to three or more masculine and feminine human groups or entities.

Example :

Plural pronoun 'm-f,p' *

English	Singular/مُفْرَد	Plural
we (1st person)	أنَا	نَحْنُ
you (2nd person)	أنتَ ، أنتِ	أنتُم
they (3rd person)	هُوَ ، هِيَ	هُم

(*) Masculine and feminine plural for three or more

- **Pronoun's suffix** ضَمِيْرٌ مُتَّصِلْ

  _ The pronoun suffix is an Arabic possessive letter or letters attached to nouns or prepositions.
  _ Each suffix corresponds to a personal pronoun (Tables 1 and 2.)
  _ When attached to the noun, the suffix creates a meaningful possessive expression.
  _ The suffix attached to the noun, a book 'm' كِتَاب, for example, the suffix expresses that the book belongs to someone (Table 3.)

_ When attached to a preposition, the suffix serves as the object of the preposition.

_ In isolation, the preposition-suffix combination has no real additional meaning (Table 4) but in the context of the sentence provides clarifying details.

Table (1) Singular possessive suffix ضَمِيْرُ التَّمَلُّكْ لِلْمُفْرَد

English	Singular possessive suffix	Singular personal pronoun
my 'm,f'	ـِي ←	أَنَا
your 'm'	ـَكَ ←	أَنْتَ
your 'f'	ـِكِ ←	أَنْتِ
his 'm'	ـهُ ←	هُوَ
her 'f'	ـها ←	هِيَ

Table (2) Plural possessive suffix ضَمِيْرُ التَّمَلُّكْ لِلْجَمْع

English	Plural possessive suffix	Plural personal pronoun
our 'm-f,p'	(our) ـنَا ←	نَحْنُ
your 'm-f,p'	(your 'f-m,p) ـكُم ←	أَنْتُم
their 'm-f,p'	(their 'f-m,p) ـهُم ←	هُم

Table (3) Possessive suffix attached to the noun
ضَمير التَّمَلُّك المُتَّصِل بالإسْم

English meaning	Suffix attached to a noun (book 'ms') كِتَاب	Pronoun suffix	Personal pronoun
my book 1st 'm-f,s'	كِتَاب /كِتَابـــي (belongs to me)	ـــي	أنا (I)
our book 1st 'm-f,p'	كِتَاب /كِتَابُـنَـا (belongs to us)	ـــنَـا	نَحْنُ (we)
your book 2nd 'ms'	كِتَاب /كِتَابُـكَ (belongs to you 'm')	ـــكَ	أنْتَ (you)
your book '2nd 'fs'	كِتَاب /كِتَابُـكِ (belongs to you 'f')	ـــكِ	أنْتِ (you, f)
your book 2nd 'm-f,p'	كِتَابُـكُم (belongs to you all)	ـــكُم	أنتُم (you, m-f,p)
his book 3rd 'ms'	كِتَابُـهُ (belongs to him 'm')	ـــهُ	هُوَ (he, m)
her book 3rd 'fs'	كِتَابُـهَا (belongs to her 'f')	ـــهَا	هِيَ (she, f)
their book 3rd 'm-f,p'	كِتَابُـهُم (belongs to them, m-f,p)	ـــهُم	هُم (they, m-f, p)

Table (4) Pronoun suffix attached to prepositions
ضَمِيْر مُتَّصِل بِحُروفِ الجَرّ

English meaning	Suffix attached to prepositions	Pronoun suffix	Propositions	Prepositions حُرُوف الجَرّ
in them 'm,f'	فِيهِم	ـهُم (them)	in	فِي
to you 'm'	إلَيْكَ	ـكَ (you 'm')	to	إلَى
to you 'f'	إلَيْكِ	ـكِ (you 'f')	to	إلَى
from him	مِنْهُ	ـهُ (him)	from	مِن
from her	مِنْها	ـها (her)	from	مِن
on us upon us	عَلَيْنا	ـنا (us)	on, upon	عَلَى
with him	مَعَهُ	ـهُ (him)	with	مَعَ
with her	مَعَها	ـها (her)	with	مَعَ
with/by you 'm,f'	بِكُم	ـكُم (you, 'm,f')	with/by	بِـ
off/away from you 'm,f'	عَنْكُم	ـكُم (you, 'm,f')	off/away from	عَن
for them 'm,f'	لَهُم	ـهُم (them, 'm,f')	to/for	لَـ

- **Demonstrative pronoun** اِسْمُ الإِشَارَة

  _ In Arabic, the demonstrative pronoun is called اِسْمُ الإِشَارَة.
  _ Its meaning is similar to English, for example, "this" هَـذَا/ هَـذِهِ.
  _ Unlike English, demonstrative pronoun, takes feminine or masculine forms based on the gender of the noun it precedes, for example, "this man" هَـذَا الرَّجُل or "this girl" هَـذِهِ البِنْت.
  _ The demonstrative pronoun can be the first part of a nominal sentence construct.
  _ Plural demonstrative pronoun has one form for both masculine and feminine human nouns.
  _ The demonstrative pronoun is a singular feminine preceding a non-human plural noun. The samples of these demonstrative pronouns can be found in Table 5:

Table 5 The demonstrative pronoun اِسْمُ الإِشَارَة

Pronouns	English meaning	Demonstrative pronouns	Demonstrative expressions	English meaning
feminine singular demonstrative	this	هَـذِهِ	هَـذِهِ صَدِيقَتِي	This is my friend
feminine singular demonstrative preceding non-human plural noun	this	هَـذِهِ	هَـذِهِ كُتُبِي هَـذِهِ مُدُن	These are my books, these are cities
masculine singular demonstrative	this	هَـذَا	هَـذَا أَخِي	This is my brother
plural masculine/ feminine demonstrative	these or those	هَـؤُلاءِ	هَـؤُلاءِ زُمَلائِي/ زَمِيلاتِي	These are my colleagues

Notes:

Test Section VII

VII-1. Fill in the blanks with the letter 'm' for masculine or 'f' for feminine next to the following singular nouns:

school	مَدرَسَة	_____
college	كُلِّيَّة	_____
street	شَارِع	_____
boy	وَلَد	_____
paper	وَرَقَة	_____
pencil	قَلَم	_____
building	بِنَايَة	_____
flower	وَرْدَة	_____
university	جَامِعَة	_____
Iraq	العِراق	_____

VII-2. Read the nouns in the first column. Place a checkmark (✓) in the box to indicate whether the noun is masculine, feminine, common, or proper. An answer choice is in the first row:

مُؤَنَّث feminine	مُذَكَّر masculine	إسْم خَاص proper	إسْم عَام common	الإسْم noun
✓		✓		مِصْر
				جَامِعَة
				مَكْتَب
				شَارِع
				بَيْت
				قِطَّة
				أَحْمَد
				رَجُل
				مَكْتَبَة
				كَلْب
				سُورِيَا
				بَاب
				سَيَّارَة
				فْلُورِيْدَا

VII-3. Fill in the blanks with masculine and feminine broken plural nouns. Label each word with 'mbp' for masculine broken plural or 'fbp' for feminine broken plural. *The first row has a sample answer:*

Singular noun	Plural noun
woman إِمْرَأَة	نِسَاء 'fbp'
كِتَاب book	
وَلَد boy	
قِطَّة cat	
كَنِيسَة church	
مَدِينَة city	
صَفّ class	
فُسْتَان dress	
قِسْم department	
أُذُن ear	
عَيْن eye	
مَصْنَع factory	
وَرْدَة flower	
حَدِيْقَة garden	

135

	تَل hill	
	بَيْت house	
	فَرْد individual	
	مَلِك king	
	رِسَالَة letter	
	رَجُل man	
	شَهْر month	
	جَبَل mountain	
	مَكْتَب office	
	قَلَم pencil	
	زَهْرَة rose	
	مَدْرَسَة school	
	بَحْر sea	
	مَخْزَن store	
	شَارِع street	
	شَجَرَة tree	

VII-4. Fill in the blanks with plural forms of the singular noun choices.
An answer choice is the first sentence.

١. في هٰذِهِ الجَامِعَة **طُلَّاب وَ طَالِبَات وَ أَسَاتِذَة وَ أُسْتَاذَات** .

❶ طَالِب ❷ طَالِبَة ❸ أُسْتَاذ ❹ أُسْتَاذَة

٢. بَغْدَاد والقَاهِرَة وبَيْروت ــــــــــــ في الشَّرْق الأَوْسَط.

❶ مَدِينَة ❷ وِلايَة ❸ بَلَد ❹ شَارِع

٣. في هٰذا الشَّارِع ــــــــــــ وَ ــــــــــــ وَ ــــــــــــ وَ ــــــــــــ .

❶ بِنَايَة ❷ جَامِعَة ❸ مَخْزَن ❹ سَيَّارَة

٤. في الجَامِعَة ــــــــــــ وَ ــــــــــــ وَ ــــــــــــ .

❶ مَكْتَبَة ❷ سَمَر ❸ مَكْتَب ❹ كَمبيُوتَر

٥. ميرِيلَاند وفْلُورِيدَا وَجُورْجْيَا ــــــــــــ في أَمْرِيكَا.

❶ وِلايَة ❷ قَرْيَة ❸ لِيبِيا ❹ أَمْرِيكَا

٦. في مَدْرَسَتِي ــــــــــــ وَ ــــــــــــ وَ ــــــــــــ .

❶ صَفّ ❷ طَاوِلَة ❸ قِطَّة ❹ كُرسِيّ

٧. في مَدِينَتِي ــــــــــــ وَ ــــــــــــ وَ ــــــــــــ .

❶ مَصْنَع ❷ مَرْكَز ❸ حَدِيقَة ❹ مَطْعَم

٨. في بَيْتي _____ وَ _____ وَ _____ .

① غُرْفَة ② شُبَّاك ③ بَاب ④ قِطَّة

٩. في مَدينَتي _____ وَ _____ وَ _____ .

① بَيْت ② مَدْرَسَة ③ حَديقَة ④ شَجَرَة

١٠. في ولايَتي _____ وَ _____ وَ _____ .

① فَرد ② نَهَر ③ جَبَل ④ تَل

VII-5. Fill in the blanks with the appropriate Arabic personal plural pronouns. Pay close attention to 1st, 2nd, or 3rd person:

Example: engineers - هم

1. Friends _____

2. Son of my uncle in the room _____

3. You, the American students _____

4. We are teachers. _____

5. Men and women _____

6. Mothers and sons and daughters _____

7. We are men. _____

8. Students to make up the class _____

9. We went to the movie. _____

10. Egyptians, Tunisians, Moroccans, and Algerians are Arabs. _____

VII-6. Underline the personal pronouns and the demonstrative pronouns in the following sentences. Translate these pronouns into Arabic. *The first sentence is a sample answer:*

- <u>He</u> is busy with translation.   هو

- Those are teachers of Arabic Language and Culture.

- You have only 20 men and women students in this class.

- These books are from the library.

- They are friends from Lebanon and Syria.

- This female student is in high school.

- This is the biggest university in the State of Maryland.

- They live in a small house in the city.

- You are a female engineering student from Kuwait.

- He is a professor who speaks the Arabic Language.

VII-7 Fill in the blanks with the following:
- In Column 3, write the possessive pronoun suffixes that correspond to the nouns in Column 1 and personal pronouns in Column 2
- In Column 4, write out the new possessive nouns
- In Column 5, write the English translation of the Arabic possessive nouns you wrote in Column 4
- *The first row contains a sample answer:*

5	4	3	2	1
English translation	**Possessive nouns**	**Possessive pronoun**	**Personal pronouns**	**Nouns**
My house	بَيْتِي	ـِي	أنا	بَيْتٌ
			هُوَ	سَيَّارَةٌ
			نَحْنُ	مَكْتَبٌ
			أنتَ	مَدْرَسَةٌ
			أنتُم	كِتَابٌ
			هُم	جَامِعَةٌ
			أنتِ	إسْمٌ
			هِيَ	غُرْفَةٌ
			نَحْنُ	كُتُبٌ
			أنا	غُرْفَةٌ
			أنتُم	شَارِعٌ

VII- 8. Fill in the blank with the suffix possessive pronoun that corresponds to the personal pronoun in quotation marks. *The first sentence is an answer choice:*

١. إمْتِحَانُ "أنْتُم" ـكُم اليَوم سَهْل.

٢. مَدْرَسَةُ "أنا" ـــــــ كَبيرة ومدْرَسَة (أنتِ) ـــــــ صغيرة.

٣. مَدِينَةُ "هم" ـــــــ في ميريلاند و مَدِينة (أنْتُم) ـــــــ في فلوريدا.

٤. جَامِعَةُ "أنْتُم" ـــــــ في العِرَاق.

٥. هَذِهِ سَيَّارَةُ "هِيَ" ـــــــ من ألمَانيا.

٦. كُتُبُ "نَحْنُ" ـــــــ في المَكْتَبَة.

٧. سَاعَةُ "أنْتَ" ـــــــ مِنَ اليابان.

٨. بَيْتُ "أنْتِ" ـــــــ في المدِينَة.

٩. صَفُّ "أنتَ" ـــــــ في هَذِه البِنَايَة البَيْضاء.

١٠. أصْحابُ "نَحْنُ" ـــــــ وأصْحابُ (أنْتُم) ـــــــ يَلْعَبُونَ كُرَة القَدَم.

141

VII-9. In the following sentences translate into English only the underlined nouns, pronouns, and demonstrative pronouns. *The first sentence contains a sample answer:*

١. <u>هٰذا</u> سَليم مع <u>والدِه</u>.   **his father**   **This,**

٢. مَشْغُولُون في <u>عَمَلِهِم</u>. _____ their work

٣. <u>هٰؤُلاء</u> <u>أَوْلادي</u>. _____ These, my children

٤. <u>بَيْتُنا</u> قَريبٌ مِن <u>كُلِّيَّتي</u>. _____ Our house, my college

٥. <u>أَنْتُم</u> في جامِعات أمريكية. _____ You

٦. <u>مَدارِسُكُم</u> بَعيدة وواسِعَة. _____ Your schools

٧. <u>هٰؤُلاء</u> عَرَب في كُلِّيَّة اللُّغات. _____ These

٨. في <u>هٰذه</u> <u>البُيُوت</u> غُرَفٌ واسِعَة. _____ these, houses

٩. <u>أَنْتَ</u> و<u>سَميرَة</u> في كُلِّيَّة اللُّغات القَديمَة. _____ You, Samira

١٠. <u>الكُتُب</u> و<u>الأَقْلام</u> مِن <u>مَخْزَن</u> <u>الكُلِّيَّة</u>. _____ The books, the pens, storeroom, the college

VII-10. Fill in the blanks with demonstrative pronouns that match the gender (masculine or feminine) and number (singular or plural) of the noun or adjective in the sentences:

١. ـــــــــــــــــــ كَلبُ صاحِبي.

٢. ـــــــــــــــــــ زَميلاتي في صَفِّ اللُّغَةِ العَرَبيَّةِ.

٣. صَديقَتي تَسكُن في ـــــــــــــــــــ البَيْتِ.

٤. ـــــــــــــــــــ السَّيّارَةُ قَديمَةٌ.

٥. ـــــــــــــــــــ الأَخْبارُ جَيِّدةٌ.

٦. ـــــــــــــــــــ بِنتٌ صَغيرَةٌ.

٧. ـــــــــــــــــــ البَناتُ والأولادُ طُلّابٌ عَرَب.

٨. ـــــــــــــــــــ الرِّجالُ عُمّالٌ في المَصنَعِ.

٩. ـــــــــــــــــــ الثِّيابُ قَديمَةٌ.

١٠. ـــــــــــــــــــ الطُّلّابُ مِنَ السُّودان.

VII-11. Determine the gender (masculine or feminine) of the nouns, pronouns, and demonstrative pronouns in the Arabic sentences in Column 2. R-write your choice either in Column 3 or Column 4. *The first row is an answer choice:*

1 English sentence	2 Arabic sentence	3 Masculine	4 Feminine
This is a door.	هٰذَا بَاب.	هٰذَا بَاب.	
This is a table.	هٰذِه طَاوِلَة.		
This is Sameer.	هٰذَا سَمِيْر.		
She is my mother.	هِيَ أُمِّي.		
It is a dog.	هُوَ كَلْب.		
This is a cat.	هٰذِه قِطَّة.		
These/those are my brothers	هٰؤُلاء إخْوَتِي.		
This is a room.	هٰذِه غُرْفَة.		
This is a sheet of paper.	هٰذِه وَرَقَة.		
This test is difficult.	هٰذَا إمْتِحَان صَعْب.		
This is a car.	هٰذِه سَيَّارَة.		

This is Mona.	هَـذِه مُنـى		
This is Ahmad.	هَـذا أَحْمَد.		
She is my friend.	هِـيَ صَدِيقَتِي		
He is my cousin	هُوَ اْبنُ عَمِّي.		
These/those are my friends.	هَـؤُلاء أَصْدِقَائِي.		

Notes:

Section VIII: Adjectives الصِّفات "assifat"

The Adjective	الصِّفَة "assifa"
The Nisba	النِّسْبَة "annisba"
The Adjective Expression	تَعْبِير الصِّفَة

In both Arabic and English, the adjective describes nouns and pronouns. Unlike English, the adjective in Arabic constantly follows the noun and agrees with the noun's number (singular or plural), gender (masculine or feminine), and vowels, except for the non-human plural nouns.

A. Types of Adjectives أنواع الصِّفات

A-1. Masculine and Feminine Singular Adjectives:

Egyptian 'm'	مِصْرِيّ	Iraqi 'm'	عِراقِيّ
beautiful 'f'	جَميلَة	engineer 'm'	مُهَنْدِس
student 'f'	طَالِبَة	student 'm'	طالِب
American 'f'	أمريكِيَّة	assistant 'm'	مُسَاعِد
accountant 'm'	مُحاسِب	teacher 'f'	مُدَرِّسَة
teacher 'm'	مُدَرِّس	advisor 'm'	مُرْشِد
professor 'f'	أسْتاذَة	volunteer 'm'	مُتَطَوِّع

A-2. Human Masculine and Feminine Plural Adjectives:

- When adjectives describe the masculine plural nouns, ون or يـن are the plural letter suffixes to change the singular masculine adjectives into their sound (regular) plural form جَمْع المُذَكَّرْ السَّالِم.
- The suffix ات changes the singular feminine adjectives into the sound (regular) feminine plural جَمْع المُؤَنَّث السَّالِم.

- Attaching the plural suffixes **ون** or **ين** or **ات** to a singular adjective references their grammatical position in a noun or a verb sentence.
- The following table is selected adjectives with suffixes **ون ، ين** and **ات**

Examples:

Singular adjective (f-m,s)	Sound Masculine Plural (smp)	Sound Feminine Plural (sfp)
Iraqi عِراقِيّ/عِراقِيّة	عِراقِيُّون/ عِراقِيِّين	عِراقِيَّات
Egyptian مِصْرِيّ/مِصْرِيَّة	مِصْرِيُّون/مِصْرِيِّين	مِصْرِيَّات
Lebanese لُبْنَانِيّ/لُبْنَانِيَّة	لُبْنَانِيُّون/لُبْنَانِيِّين	لُبْنَانِيَّات
American أمريكِيّ/ أمريكِيَّة	أمريكِيُّون/ أمريكِيِّين	أمريكِيَّات
advisor مُرْشِد /مُرْشِدَة	مُرْشِدُون/مُرْشِدِين	مُرْشِدَات
engineer مُهَنْدِس/ مُهَنْدِسَة	مُهَنْدِسُون/ مُهَنْدِسِين	مُهَنْدِسَات
teacher مُدَرِّس /مُدَرِّسَة	مُدَرِّسُون/ مُدَرِّسِين	مُدَرِّسَات
volunteer مُتَطَوِّع/مُتَطَوِّعَة	مُتَطَوِّعُون/ مُتَطَوِّعِين	مُتَطَوِّعَات

A-3. Adjectives for pronouns and demonstrative pronouns:

When an adjective describes a pronoun or a demonstrative pronoun, it constructs a useful noun sentence.

Example:

I am an engineer. 'fs'	أنا مُهَنْدِسَة.
We are workers. 'mp'	نَحْنُ عُمَّال.
You are an American. 'ms'	أنتَ أمْريكِيّ.
You are an American. 'fs'	أنتِ أمْريكِيَّة.
You are doctors. 'mp'	أنتم أطِبّاء.
He is Moroccan. 'ms'	هُو مَغْرِبِيّ.
He is a student. 'ms'	هو طَالِب.
She is a student. 'fs'	هي طَالِبَة.
He is a teacher. 'ms'	هو مُدَرِّس.
She is a professor. 'fs'	هي أُسْتاذَة.
They are Iraqis. 'm-f,p'	هم عِراقِيُّون/ عِراقِيَّات.
You are teachers. 'm-f,p'	أنتم مُدرِّسُون/ مُدرِّسَات.
We are engineers. 'fp'	نَحْنُ مُهَنْدِسَات.
This is my friend 'fs'	هٰذهِ صَديقَتي.
This is my colleague. 'ms'	هٰذا زَميلي.
These/those are professors. 'm-f,p'	هٰؤلاء أسَاتِذَة/ أسْتاذات.

A-4. Adjectives for non-human plural nouns:

When adjectives describe plural masculine and feminine non-human nouns, the adjective form is feminine singular.

Example:

Singular non-human noun	Plural non-human noun 'fp'	Singular feminine adjective	Plural noun adjective
school مَدْرَسَة	schools مَدَارِس	vocational مِهَنِيَّة	مَدَارِس مِهَنِيَّة
tree شَجَرَة	trees أَشْجَار	green خَضْرَاء	أَشْجَار خَضْرَاء
book كِتَاب	books كُتُب	old قَدِيْمَة	كُتُب قَدِيْمَة
picture صُوْرَة	pictures صُوَر	beautiful جَمِيْلَة	صُوَر جَمِيْلَة
car سَيَّارَة	cars سَيَّارَات	big كَبِيْرَة	سَيَّارَات كَبِيْرَة
street شَارِع	streets شَوَارِع	wide وَاسِعَة	شَوَارِع وَاسِعَة
store مَخْزَن	stores مَخَازِن	small صَغِيْرَة	مَخَازِن صَغِيْرَة
market سُوق	markets أَسْوَاق	diverse مُتَنَوِّعَة	أَسْوَاق مُتَنَوِّعَة
house بَيْت	houses بُيُوْت	new جَدِيْدَة	بُيُوْت جَدِيْدَة
chair كُرْسِيّ	chairs كَرَاسِي	black سَوْدَاء	كَرَاسِي سَوْدَاء

B. Types of Nisba Adjective   أنواع صِفَات النِّسبَة

B-1. The Human Nisba Adjective

The Nisba Adjective is a specifically gendered adjective that references mainly the ethnic human background, nationality, a specialty of a human noun, or the origin of a non-human product. To construct this type of adjective, attach the following letter suffixes to the masculine and feminine adjectives:

"ي" is the masculine suffix for the singular Nisba adjective

"ـية" is the feminine suffix for the singular Nisba adjective

"ون" is the plural masculine suffix of a Nisba adjective in a noun or verb sentence, (details in sections X and XI)

"ين" is the plural masculine suffix of a Nisba adjective object to a conjugated verb (details in section XI)

"ين" is the plural masculine suffix of a Nisba adjective preceded by a preposition

"ات" is the plural feminine suffix for the Nisba adjective

Example:

The Country of origin is Syria "سُورْيا"

- To form a masculine singular Nisba adjective drop " يّ " and " ا " from the name of the country سُورْيا
- Attach suffix " يّ " to سُور
- The new Nisba adjective is (سُورِيّ.) Pronounce it.

- To form a feminine singular Nisba adjective drop the " يّ " and "ا" from the name of the country سُورْيا

- Attach suffixes " يّــة " to سُور

- The new Nisba adjective is (سُورِيَّــة.) Pronounce it.

- To form the masculine plural Nisba adjective drop the "ا" from the name of the country سُورْيا

- Attach " ون " or " ين " to سُورِيّ

- Pronounce the new Nisba adjective as (سُورِيُّــون/سُورِيِّــين)

- To form the feminine plural Nisba adjective attach suffixes ات to masculine singular سُورِيّ. Pronounce the new Nisba adjective as (سُورِيَّات)

- To form the masculine and feminine Nisba adjective of a country defined with ' the ' " الـ " such as Saudi Arabia " الـسُّعُودِيَّـة ", drop these 2 letters and the letter " ة ." The new Nisba adjective is ('ms' سُعُودِيّ.) Attach suffix " ة " to the masculine singular سُعُودِيّ. Pronounce the new Nisba adjective as ('fs' سُعُودِيَّة.)

The table below displays the different forms of selected singular and plural nationality Nisba adjectives:

Example:

Country	Feminine Plural	Masculine Plural	Nisba Adjective 'f-m,s'
الـسُّعُودِيَّة Saudi Arabia	سُعُودِيَّات	سُعُودِيُّون/سُعُودِيِّــين	سُعُودِيّ/ سُعُودِيَّة
الإمارات Emirates	إماراتِيَّات	إماراتِيُّون/إماراتِيِّــين	إماراتِيّ/إماراتِيَّة

151

مَغْرِبيّ/مَغْرِبيّة	مَغْرِبيُّون/مَغْرِبيِّين	مَغْرِبيّات	المَغْرِب Morocco
أمْريكيّ/أمْريكيّة	أمْريكيُّون/أمْريكيِّين	أمْريكيّات	أمْريكا America
قَطَريّ/قَطَريّة	قَطَريُّون/قَطَريِّين	قَطَريّات	قَطَر Qatar
فِرَنْسيّ/فِرَنْسيّة	فِرَنْسيُّون/فِرَنْسيِّين	فِرَنْسيّات	فِرَنْسا France
سُودانيّ/سُودانيّة	سُودانيُّون/سُودانيِّين	سُودانيّات	السُّودان Sudan
عِراقيّ/عِراقيّة	عِراقيُّون/عِراقيِّين	عِراقيّات	العِراق Iraq

B-2. Exception: Some masculine plural Nisba adjectives form are without ون or ين suffixes.

Example:

Arabs are not عَرَبيُّون/عَرَبيِّين but عَرَب

Indians are not هِنْديُّون/هِنْديِّين but هُنود

Turks are not تُركيُّون/تُركيِّين but أتْراك

Kurds are not كُرْديُّون/كُرْديِّين but أكْراد

Exception: Africans' Nisba adjective is either إفْريقيُّون/إفْريقيِّين or أفَارِقة

- The letter suffixes "ي", "يــة", and "ون" or, "ين" may be used to form the Nisba adjective of a profession such as :
- University professor 'ms' (جَامِعِيّ) أُسْتاذ or 'fs' (جَامِعِيَّة) أُسْتاذَة
    o Masculine plural 'mp' (جَامِعِيُّون) أَسَاتِذَة, or (جَامِعِيِّين)
    o Feminine plural 'fp' (جَامِعِيَّات) أُسْتاذَات
- A diplomat 'ms' (دِبْلُومَاسِيّ) or 'fs' (دِبْلُومَاسِيَّة)
    o Masculine plural 'mp' دِبْلُومَاسِيُّون/ دِبْلُومَاسِيِّين
    o Feminine plural 'fp' دِبْلُومَاسِيَّات
- A village dweller, a villager 'ms' (قَرَوِيّ) or 'fs' (قَرَوِيَّة)
    o Masculine plural 'mp' قَرَوِيُّون/ قَرَوِيِّين
    o Feminine plural 'fp' قَرَوِيَّات
- The origin of a product
    o An American car 'fs' سَيَّارَة أَمْرِيكِيَّة
    o Feminine plural 'fp' سَيَّارَات أَمْرِيكِيَّة

B-3. The Non-Human Nisba Adjective

The Nisba adjective for a non-human feminine plural noun is a feminine singular Nisba adjective.

Example:

Egyptian cities	مُدُن مِصرِيَّة
American universities	جَامِعَات أمريكِيَّة
Japanese cars	سَيَّارَات يابانِيَّة

German telephones	هَوَاتِف أَلْمَانِيَّة
African jungles	غَابَات إِفْرِيقِيَّة
English books	كُتُب إِنْجِلِيزِيَّة
Arabian horses	حُصُن عَرَبِيَّة
Foreign languages	لُغَات أَجْنَبِيَّة
Italian shoes	أَحْذِيَة إِيْطَالِيَّة
French clothing	مَلَابِس فِرَنْسِيَّة

C. Adjective expression (Sifa expression) تَعْبِير الصِّفَة

Sifa expression (تَعْبِير الصِّفَة) is a combination of an interrelated defined noun and defined adjective. In English, adjectives precede the noun they describe. For example "the **beautiful** girl", "the **new** house", or "the **red** car" form adjective expressions or phrases. In Arabic, this construct is reversed. The adjective comes after the noun to form an expression or a phrase. For example, البِنْتُ الجَمِيلَةُ translates as the "girl the beautiful, البيتُ الجَديدُ the "house the new", and السَّيَّارَةُ الحَمْرَاءُ the "car the red". The Sifa expression's only function is to complete or complement useful noun or verb sentences. *More details are in sections (X and XI.)*

Types of adjective expression أنواع تَعْبِير الصِّفَة

- The adjective expression is a two-term construct. The first term is always a definite noun. The second term is always a definite adjective.
- The adjective always follows the noun it describes instead of preceding it.
- Unlike English, the adjective always agrees with the gender of the noun, its number, and its vowels.

The following are types of adjective expressions:

C-1. When the first term noun is defined with the prefix 'the' " الـ ", the second term adjective follows prefixed with " الـ " and shares its gender as well.

Examples:

The girl the beautiful/the beautiful girl 'f'	الـبِنْتُ الـجَمِيلَةُ
The friend the Arab/the Arab friend 'f'	الـصَّدِيقَةُ الـعَرَبِيَّةُ
The house the big/the big house 'm'	الـبَيْتُ الـكَبِيرُ
The building the high/the high building 'f'	الـبِنَايَةُ الـعَالِيَةُ

C-2. The first term of the adjective phrase is an adjective and the second term is feminine or masculine singular or plural, the phrase terms are defined with " الـ.".

Examples:

the sister the young/the young sister 'fs'	الأختُ الصَّغِيرَةُ
the older the brother/the older brother 'm'	الأخُ الكَبِيرُ
the mothers the dear/the dear mothers 'fp'	الأمَّهاتُ العَزِيزاتُ
the students the successful/the successful students 'mp'	الطُّلَّابُ النَّاجِحُونَ

C-3. The noun is masculine singular, the adjective is masculine singular. The noun is feminine singular, the adjective is feminine singular.

Examples:

the window the wide/the wide window 'ms'	الشُّبَّاكُ الواسِعُ
the door the white/the white door 'ms'	البَابُ الأبْيَضُ
the room the spacious/ the spacious room 'fs'	الغُرْفَةُ الكَبِيرَةُ
the tree the green/the green tree 'fs'	الشَّجَرَةُ الخَضْراءُ

C-4. The noun is definite feminine non-human plural, the adjective is definite feminine singular.

Examples:

the cities the Arabic/the Arabic cities   المُدُنُ العَرَبيَّةُ

the cars the Japanese/ the Japanese cars   السَّيَّاراتُ اليَابانِيَّةُ

the universities the American/ the American universities   الجَامِعَاتُ الأمريكيَّةُ

the building the historical/the historical building   البِنَايَاتُ التَّأريخِيَّةُ

C-5. The masculine or feminine adjective agrees with the noun's vowel.

Examples:

the book the new/the new college

fatHa) فَتْحَة) الكِتابَ الجَديدَ /الكُلِّيَّة الجَديدَة

the book the new/the new college

kasra) كَسْرَة) الكِتابِ الجَديدِ /الكُلِّيَّة الجَديدَةِ

the book the new/the new college

damma) ضَمَّة) الكِتابُ الجَديدُ /الكُلِّيَّة الجَديدَةُ

C-6. The adjective agrees with the undefined noun nunation vowels, double fatHa, double kasra, double damma

Examples:

the building, the high/ The high building 'fs'   بِنَايَةً عَالِيَةً

the building, the high/ The high building 'fs'   بِنايَةٍ عَالِيَةٍ

the building, the high/ The high building 'fs'   بِنايَةٌ عَالِيَةٌ

C-7. When the noun is a proper noun, the adjective is definite with " الـ."

Examples:

America the north /the north America   أمريكَا الشَّمَالِيَّةُ

Ahmed the student/the student Ahmed   أحمَدُ الطَّالِبُ

Reem the Egyptian/the Egyptian Reem   رِيْمُ المِصرِيَّةُ

مُنَىٰ الدُّكْتُورَةُ	Mona the doctor/the doctor Mona

C-8. When the noun is attached to a possessive pronoun suffix, the adjective is definite with "الـ."

Examples:

مَدرَسَتُهُ الجَديدَةُ	his school the new /his new school
كُلِّيَّتُها البَعيدَةُ	her college the far away /her far away college
كِتَابي العَرَبِيُّ	my book the Arabic /my Arabic book
بُيُوتُهُم القَديمَةُ	their houses the old /their old houses

C-9. When the feminine or masculine demonstrative pronoun precedes the adjective phrase, both terms are definite with "الـ."

Examples:

هٰذِهِ السَّيَّارَةُ الكَهرَبائِيَّةُ	this the car the electric /this electric car
هٰذِهِ الكُلِّيَّةُ الجَديدَةُ	this the college the new /this new college
هٰذا أبي الطَّيِّبُ	this my father the nice /this my nice father

these/those my colleagues the Saudis/these/those my Saudi colleagues

هٰؤُلاءِ الزُّمَلاءُ السُّعُودِيُّون

C-10. When the Preposition precedes the feminine or masculine adjective, the phrase terms are defined with "الـ."

Examples:

في المَدارِسِ الجَديدةِ	**in** the new schools
علىٰ الشَّجَرةِ الخَضراءِ	**on** the tree the green/on the green tree
مع الصَّديقةِ العَرَبِيَّةِ	**wit**h my friend the Arab/with my Arab friend

from the street the <u>narrow</u> **to** the house the small/ **from** the narrow street **to** the small house

مِنَ الشَّارِعِ الضَّيِّقِ إلىٰ البَيْتِ الصَّغيرِ

Notes:

Test Section VIII

VIII-1. Fill in the blanks with the missing singular and plural feminine or masculine adjective and/or Nisba adjective. Add the gender suffixes you learned. *The first row contains a sample answer:*

Masculine singular	Masculine plural	Feminine singular	Feminine plural
مُدَرِّس Teacher	مُدَرِّسون/مُدَرِّسين	مُدَرِّسة	مُدَرِّسات
عِرَاقِيّ Iraqi			
مَغْرِبِيّ Moroccan			
مُهَنْدِس Engineer			
مُمَرِّض Nurse			
مُحَاسِب Accountant			
جَزَائِرِيّ Algerian			
تُونِسِيّ Tunisian			
مُسَافِر traveler			
أَمْرِيكِيّ American			
مُجْتَهِد Hard working			
عَرَبِيّ an Arab			

VIII-2. Fill in the blanks:

- The missing countries in Column **1**.
- The masculine and feminine Nisba adjectives in Columns **2** and **3**.
- *The first row contains a sample answer:*

1 Country	2 Singular Feminine Nisba adjective	3 Singular Masculine Nisba adjective
الأُرْدُن	أُرْدُنِيَّة	أُرْدُنِيّ
العِرَاق		
السُّعُودِيَّة		
		فِرَنْسِيّ
تُونِس		
		مِصْرِيّ
اليَابَان		
الإِمَارَات العَرَبِيَّة المُتَّحِدَة		إِمَارَاتِيّ
لُبْنَان		
	أَمْرِيْكِيَّة	
المَغْرِب		
إِنْجِلْتِرَا*		إِنْجِلِيْزِيّ*

*Nisba for England is "إِنْجِلِيْزِيّ".

VIII-3. Form feminine and masculine plural Nisba from the following masculine singular adjectives. Add the gender suffixes you learned. *The first row is a sample answer:*

Singular	Feminine Plural	Masculine Plural
مِصْرِيّ	مِصْرِيَّات	مِصْرِيُّون/ مِصْرِيِّين
تُرْكِيّ		
لِيبِيّ		
جَزَائِرِيّ		
كُوَيْتِيّ		
هِنْدِيّ		
مَكْسِيكِيّ		
عَرَبِيّ		
كَنَدِيّ		
يَمَنِيّ		

VIII-4. Complete the following sentences with the Nisba adjective form of the country in brackets. Use the correct gender suffixes.

١. هَـذا صَدِيقِي سَمِير هُوَ ـــــــــــــــ . (الكُوَيْت)

٢. هِيَ طَالِبَة جَامِعِيَّة ـــــــــــــــ . (الأُرْدُن)

٣. زُمَلائِي فِي الكُلِّيَّة عَرَب ـــــــــــــــ . (السَّعُودِيَّة)

٤. أَنْتُنَّ أُستاذات ـــــــــــــــ ـــــــــــــــ . (مِصْر ، جامِعَة)

٥. أَنْتِ تَدْرُسِين فِي جَامِعَة ـــــــــــــــ . (فَرَنْسَا)

٦. عِنْدِي سَيَّارَة ـــــــــــــــ . (اليَابَان)

٧. أَكْتُبُ رِسَالَةً إِلَى صَدِيقَة ـــــــــــــــ . (أَمْرِيكَا)

٨. أَمِين وَأَصْدِقَاؤُهُ ـــــــــــــــ (الهِنْد) يَدْرُسُون فِي المَكْتَبَة.

٩. هُوَ طَالِب ـــــــــــــــ (العِرَاق) وَهِيَ أَيْضاً طَالِبَة ـــــــــــــــ . (العِرَاق)

١٠. أُسْتَاذُ اللُّغَةِ العَرَبِيَّةِ ـــــــــــــــ . (سُورْيَا)

١١. هَلْ هُوَ طَالِب ـــــــــــــــ (رُوسْيَا)؟ لا هُوَ طَالِب ـــــــــــــــ . (لِيبْيَا)

١٢. المُدَرِّسُون فِي كُلِّيَتِنَا ـــــــــــــــ و ـــــــــــــــ و ـــــــــــــــ . (كَنَدا، فَرَنْسَا ، تُونِس)

VIII-5. Fill in the blanks of columns 2 and 3 with the appropriate Arabic Nisba adjectives for the adjective phrases in column 1. *The first row is a sample answer:*

1 Place/country and profession adjective phrase	2 Arabic Nisba	3 Arabic Nisba phrase
the university student 'ms'	الجَامِعِيُّ	الطَّالِبُ الجَامِعِيُّ
the university student 'fs'		
the university students 'm-f,p'		
the university students 'fp'		
the Japanese professor 'ms'		
the Japanese professor 'fs'		
the Japanese professors 'm-f,p'		
the Japanese professors 'fp'		

VIII-6. Fill in the blanks with the words that best fit the instructions below:

- defined or undefined
- feminine or masculine
- singular or plural adjective phrase

The first row is a sample answer:

Defined/ Undefined noun	Masculine/ Feminine noun	Singular/plural	Adjective phrase
defined	masculine	singular	الأسْتاذُ الجَديدُ
			الطَّالِبَةُ العَرَبِيَّةُ
			الطَّالِباتُ الجَديداتُ
			الرِّجالُ المِصرِيُّون
			واجِبٌ سَهْلٌ
			الرَّجُلُ الطَّيِّبُ
			مَدْرَسَةٌ صَغيرَةٌ
			أُخْتي الكَبيرَةُ
			المَكْتَبُ الهَنْدَسِيُّ
			مكْتَبَةٌ واسِعَةٌ
			النِّساءُ المَغْرِبِيّاتُ

VIII-7. Choose an appropriate adjective from Table **1** to fill in the blanks of Table **2** with the best meaningful adjective phrase. The *1ˢᵗ row of Table **2** contains a sample answer:*

Table 1				
صَعْباً	الجَميلَةُ	واسِعَةٍ	الأبْيَضُ	الجَديدُ
العَرَبِيَّةُ	العَرَبِيُّ	البَعيدَةُ	الأخْضَرُ	المِصْريّون

Table 2	
الشَّجَرُ الأخْضَرُ	الشَّجَرُ
	البِنْتُ
	الكُتُبُ
	جامِعَةٍ
	البَيْتُ
	إمْتِحاناً
	الأساتِذَةُ
	الثَّوْبُ
	الصَّديْقُ
	المَدْرَسَةُ

VIII-8. Rearrange each group of words to form a meaningful adjective phrase that agrees in gender, quantity, and vowels.

١. الأمْرِيكِيّ ـ هٰذا ـ الجَدِيدُ ـ الأسْتَاذُ

٢. تُونِسْيٌّ ـ مُوَظَّفٌ ـ هٰذا ، العِرَاقِيَّة ـ المُدَرِّسَة ـ هٰذِهِ

٣. السُّعُودِيّ ـ الطَّالِب

٤. الصَّغِيرة ـ البِنْت

٥. الأبْيَض ـ الوَاسِع ـ البَاب

٦. المِصْرِيّ ـ الأسْتَاذ

٧. قَدِيمَة ـ وَجَدِيدَة ـ سَيَّارَات

٨. السُّورِيَّة ـ المَدِينَة ـ دِمَشْق

٩. الواسِعَة ـ المَكْتَبَة ـ البَعِيدة

١٠. الأمْرِيكِيَّة ـ المُدَرِّسَة

VIII-9. Translate the following English adjective phrases into Arabic.

1. my beautiful mother

2. the kind brothers

3. my new university

4. the new building

5. the beautiful girls

6. your new car

7. their old house

8. the new teacher 'f'

9. her Arabic book

10. his difficult homework

11. her Indian friend

12. your American friend 'fs'

13. the long river

14. the Arabian coffee

VIII-10. Select a color adjective from the word bank in Table **1** to fit the best meaningful noun-color phrase in the blanks of Table **2**. Be sure that the noun and color agree in gender. *The first row of Table 2 contains a sample answer:*

Table 1 Color adjective vocabulary:

English	Masculine	Feminine
Black	أَسْوَد	سَوْداء
Blue	أَزْرَق	زَرْقاء
Brown	بُنِّيّ	بُنِّيّة
Green	أَخْضَر	خَضْراء
Orange	بُرْتُقالِيّ	بُرْتُقالِيَّة
Pink	وَرْدِيّ	وَرْدِيَّة
Purple	بَنَفْسَجِيّ	بَنَفْسَجِيَّة
Red	أَحْمَر	حَمْراء
White	أَبْيَض	بَيْضاء
Yellow	أَصْفَر	صَفْراء

Table 2 Noun and color adjective phrases:

Adjective phrases	list of Nouns
البَاب الأسوَد	البَاب
	المَوز
	التُّفَاحَة
	الزُّهُور
	الشَّجَرة
	السَّمَاء
	الوَرْدَة
	البُرتْقال
	الجَوْز "walnuts"
	الثَّوب

Notes

Section IX: Idafa Phrase

تَعْبِيرُ الإضَافَة

The Idafa phrase in Arabic is a possessive construct that combines two mutually related nouns or adjectives to complete or complement a sentence. For example, "the *book of the student/ the student's book*" is كِتَابُ ألطَّالِبِ in Arabic.

A. Types of Idafa phrases:

- The Idafa phrase is comprised of two noun terms. The 1st term is called in Arabic 'mudaf' مُضَاف which means "to add to." The 2nd term is called 'mudaf ilayhi' مُضَاف إلَيْه which means "added to it."

- The first term is always an indefinite noun or adjective. The second term can be definite, indefinite, proper, possessive, or compounded (containing more than one Idafa phrase.)

- In Arabic the function of Idafa expression (تَعْبِير) or semi-sentence phrase (شُبْه جُمْلَة), is only to make a noun or verb sentence useful. Details are in sections (IX and X)

- The following are examples of Idafa expressions:

A-1. The first term in an Idafa phrase is an indefinite noun; the second term is a definite noun where the Arabic definite article is أ ل :

Examples:

lesson of the language /the language lesson	دَرْسُ ألـلُّـغَة
library of the university /the university library	مَكْتَبَةُ ألـجَامِعَة
school of the village /the village school	مَدْرَسَةُ ألـقَرْيَة
home of the family /the family home	بَيْتُ ألـعَائِلَة

A-2. The first term is an indefinite adjective; the second term is an indefinite adjective :

Examples:

son of paternal brother /uncle's son	إبْنُ عَمّ
sons of paternal brother /uncle's sons	أبْنَاءُ عَمّ
daughter of maternal brother /uncle's daughter	إبْنَةُ خَالْ
maternal sister /aunt's daughters	بَنَاتُ خَالة

A-3. The first term is an indefinite common noun; the second term is a proper noun:

Examples:

College of Maryam /Maryam's college	كُلِّيَّةُ مَرْيَم
Company of Ahmed /Ahmad's company	شَرِكَةُ أحْمَد
University of Qatar/Qatar university	جَامِعَةُ قَطَر

A-4. The first term is an indefinite noun; the second term is defined as attached to a possessive suffix:

Examples:

the door of my house /my house door	بابُ بَيْتِي
school of my brother /my brother's school	مَدْرَسَةُ أخِي
street of our college /our college street	شَارِعُ كُلِّيَّتِنَا
family of his friend /his friend's family	أُسْرَةُ صَدِيقِهِ
car of her father/her father's car	سَيَّارَةُ وَالِدِهَا

A-5. The first term is an indefinite adjective; the second term is **compounded** Idafa الإضافة المُرَكَّبة:

Examples:

Professor of the Arabic language class	أُسْتَاذَةُ صَفّ اللُّغَةِ العَرَبِيَّةِ
Student of the College of Sciences	طَالِبَةُ كُلِّيَّةِ العُلُومِ
Student of the Department of Languages	طَالِبُ قِسْمِ اللُّغَاتِ
Engineer of the car company	مُهَنْدِسُ شَرِكَةِ السَّيَّارَاتِ

Notes:

Test Section IX

IX-1. The following are instructions to guide you:

1. Choose the combination of the first and second term nouns or adjectives from the word bank in **Tables 1** and **2** that form the most meaningful Idafa phrases.
2. Attach the definite prefixes and possessive suffixes you learned.
3. Use each word only once.
4. Fill in the blanks of your answer choice in **Table 3**:

Table 1 The first term of Idafa

كُلِّيَّةٌ	سَيَّارَةٌ	مَدِينَةٌ	صَفٌّ	بَابٌ
صَدِيقَةٌ	كِتَابٌ	شَرِكَةٌ	مَكْتَبٌ	رَئِيسٌ

Table 2 The second term of Idafa

تُوُيُوتا	عَرَبِيّ	مُدِيرٍ	أخ	جَامِعَة
أُخْت	عُلُوم	كُوَيْت	هَنْدَسَة	بَيْت

Table 3 The Idafa phrases

.٦	.١
.٧	.٢
.٨	.٣
.٩	.٤
.١٠	.٥

IX-2. Form the most meaningful Idafa phrases that best fill in the blanks. *The first row contains a sample answer:*

3	2	1
كُلِّيَّةُ الهَنْدَسَة	القَلبِ heart	كُلِّيَّةُ
	مَيريلانَد	مَدِينَةٌ
	مَكتَبِ الشَّرِكَة	أُستاذٌ
	صَديقي	جامِعَةٌ
	اللُّغَةِ العَرَبيَّةِ	كِتابٌ
	جَدَّتي	وِلايَةٌ
	الهَنْدَسَة	طَبيبٌ physician
	صَديقَتي	والِدُ
	عَمِّي ياسين	إبنٌ
	اللُّغَةِ الفِرَنْسيَّة	بَيتٌ
	فلوريدا	والِدَةٌ
	نيويورك	مُديرٌ

175

IX-3. When deciding which Idafa noun is best, fill in the blanks for each answer choice:

التَّكْنُلُوجْيَا	الصِّيَانَة	خَالِي	الهَنْدَسَة
technology	maintenance	uncle	engineering
مَرْكَز	اللُّغَات	اللُّغَة	خَالَتِي
center	languages	language	aunt

أنَا إسْمِي كَرِيْم. أسْكُن في بَيْت _____ . وأدْرُس في كُلِّيَةِ

_____ . خَالِي أُسْتَاذ _____ في الكُلِّيَّة. إبنُ خَالِي

يَدرُس _____ العَرَبِيَّة في قِسْمِ (*) _____ . إبْنَة _____

تَسكُن مَعنا وَهي طَالِبَة في _____ الحَاسُوب (**) أنا أعْمَل في

مَكْتَب _____ مَعَ زَمِيْلِي شَرِيْف.

(*) department   (**) the computer

IX-4. Translate the following English phrases into Arabic Idafa phrases:

1. Work of my son

2. Book of the student

3. Telephone of my mother

4. Restaurant of the university

5. The door of the office of the judge (الحَاكِم)

6. Brother of his American uncle

7. Book of my mother's friend 'fs'

8. Building of my friend's office

9. House of the son of my father's brother

10. Manager of the department of the Language of Arabic

IX-5. Identify the Idafa phrases in the sentences in Column **1**. Rewrite them in Column **2**. *The first row contains a sample answer:*

2	1
مَصْنَعِ ٱلسَّيَّارَاتِ	يَعْمَلُ أخي في **مَصْنَعِ ٱلسَّيَّارَاتِ**.
	القِصَّةُ في ٱلدَّرسِ ٱلأَوَّلِ هِيَ قِصَّةُ مُنَى.
	زَمِيلِي يَكْتُبُ حُروفَ ٱللُّغَةِ ٱلعَرَبِيَّةِ.
	يَأكُلُ صَدِيقي في مَطْعَمِ لُبْنَان
	أنا أسْكُنُ في بِنَايَةِ عَمِّي.
	أُختي تَلْعَبُ كُرَةَ ٱلسَّلَّةِ. basketball
	كُلِّيَّةُ ٱلعلومِ في بِنَايَةِ ٱلجَامِعَةِ.
	مَدِينَةُ نْيُويُورْك في وِلايَةِ نْيُويُورْك.
	أسْكُنُ مَعَ جَدَّةِ أولادِي في وِلايَةِ ميريلاند
	فِي ٱللُّغَةِ ٱلعَرَبِيَّةِ تَعبيرُ ٱلصِّفَةِ وَٱلإضَافَةِ.

IX-6 Select the two terms of Idafa phrases from the following word sets. Rewrite them. *For the word set number one, a sample answer is in bold:*

١. فَصْل ـ جَمِيلَة ـ رُوكْفِيل ـ ألصَّيف ـ مَدِينَة ـ في

فَصْلُ الصَّيفِ ـ مَدِينَةُ رُوكْفيل

٢. ألعَمّ ـ عَن ـ بَعِيدٌ ـ بَيتُ ـ كُلِّيَّتِي

٣. صَدِيقِي ـ وَالِدةُ ـ تُشَاهِدُ ـ وَالِدَتِي ـ مَعَ ـ ألتِّلفَاز

٤. مَدرَسَةِ ـ في ـ أُختِي ـ ألبَنَاتِ ـ ألإبتِدَائِيَّةِ

٥. في ـ أخِي ـ يَدْرُسُ ـ كُلِّيَّتِهِ ـ مَعَ ـ ألبَعِيدَةِ ـ صَدِيقِهِ

٦. في ـ ثَانَوِيَّةٍ ـ إبنُ ـ مَدرَسَةٍ ـ صَدِيقَتِي

٧. أُمِّي ـ خَالَتِي ـ أُختُ ـ وَأُختُ ـ عَمَّتِي ـ وَالِدِي

٨. ألتِّلفَاز ـ ألأخبَارِ ـ ألقِصَّةِ ـ على ـ صُوَرُ ـ في

٩. اللُّغَةِ العَرَبِيَّةِ ـ سَمِير ـ وَاجِبُ ـ يَكْتُبُ

١٠. قِطَّةُ ـ بَيتِنَا ـ في ـ صَاحِبَتِي

Notes

Section X: The Nominal (Noun) Sentence

الجُمْلَة الإسْمِيَّة

A functional noun sentence الجُمْلَة الإسْمِيَّة in Arabic is similar in construct to those in English. For example," The student is American", in Arabic translates only into two words: الطَّالِبُ أمريكِيٌّ.

The noun sentence is composed of two essential parts: The first part is the beginning of the sentence which is the **subject** المُبْتَدَأ, and the second part is the **predicate** الخَبَر which is the information about the subject necessary to complete the useful sentence.

A. Combinations of types of subjects and predicates

أنْواع المُبْتَدَأ وَالخَبَر

A-1. The subject is a definite singular common noun, and the predicate is an indefinite singular adjective:

Examples:

The house is "big."	البَيْتُ "كَبيرٌ."
The girl is "intelligent."	البِنْتُ "ذَكِيَّةٌ."
The car is "ancient."	السَّيَّارَةُ "قَديمَةٌ."

A-2. The subject is a proper noun (For example, Sarah, Esam, Angela), and the predicate is an indefinite adjective:

Examples:

"Sarah" is a student.	"سَارَه" طَالِبَةٌ.
"Esam" is a professor.	"عِصَامُ" أسْتاذٌ.
"Angela" is a doctor.	"آنْجِلَا" دُكْتُورَةٌ.

A-3. The subject is a personal pronoun, and the predicate is an indefinite adjective:

Examples:

"He" is a physician.	"هو" طَبيبٌ.
"I" am sick.	"أنـا" مَريضٌ.
"We" are Americans	"نَحْنُ" أمريكِيُّون.

A-4. The subject is a personal pronoun, and the predicate is a preposition Phrase:

Examples:

She is "in the house."	هِيَ "في البَيتِ."
They are "in the university".	هُم "في الجامِعَةِ."
You are "in the classroom."	أنْتُم "في الصَّفِ."

A-5. The subject is a proper noun, and the predicate is a noun sentence:

Examples:

George "he is a student."	جُورْج "هُوَ طالِبٌ."
Sarah "she is a nurse."	سارَه "هِيَ مُمَرِّضَةٌ."
Ahmed "he is a hard worker."	أحْمَد "هُوَ مُجْتَهِدٌ."

A-6. The subject is an adjective phrase, and the predicate is an indefinite adjective:

Examples:

"The new student" is an Arab.	"الطَّالِبُ الجَديدُ" عَرَبِيٌّ.
"The Arab girl" is my friend.	"البِنْتُ العَرَبِيَّةُ" صَديقَتِي.
"The old dress" is white.	"الثَّوبُ القَديمُ" أبيَضٌ.

A-7. The subject is an adjective phrase, and the predicate is a preposition phrase:

Examples:

The new student is "from Yemen."	الطَّالِبَةُ الجَدِيدَةُ "مِن اليَمَن."
The American professor is in the library"	الأسْتاذُ الأمْرِيكِيُّ "في المَكْتَبَة."
The red flower is "on the table."	الوَرْدَةُ الحَمْراءُ "عَلَىٰ الطَّاوِلَة."

A-8. The subject is an Idafa phrase, and the predicate is an adjective:

Examples:

"The manager of the factory" is an engineer.	"مُدِيرُ المَصْنَعِ" مُهَنْدِسٌ.
"The car of my brother" is new.	"سَيَّارَةُ أخِي" جَدِيدَةٌ.
"The building of the university" is far.	"بِنايَةُ الجامِعَةِ" بَعِيدَةٌ.

A-9. The subject has a possessive pronoun suffix, and the predicate is a preposition and an Idafa phrase:

Examples:

My book is "from the college store."	كِتابِي "مِن مَخْزَنِ الكُلِّيَّةِ."
Our book is "from the college library."	كِتابُنا "مِن مَكْتَبَةِ الكُلِّيَّةِ."
Your lesson is "in the chemistry class".	دَرْسُكَ "فِي صَفِّ الكِيمْياءِ."
Your homework is "in the physics class "	واجِبُكِ "فِي صَفِّ الفِيزِياءِ."
Your lesson is" in the college lab."	دَرْسُكُم "فِي مُخْتَبَرِ الكُلِّيَّةِ."
His book is "at Ahmad's house ."	كِتابُهُ "فِي بَيْتِ أحْمَد."
Her dress is "from the city of Paris."	ثَوْبُها "مِن مَدِينَةِ بارِيس."

A-10. The subject is a proper or common noun, and the predicate is an adverb phrase:

Examples:

Semer is "at the front door."	سَمَر "أمامَ البابِ."
The book is "on top of the shelf."	الكِتابُ "فَوْقَ الرَّفِ."
The dog is "behind the fence."	الكَلْبُ "وَراءَ السِّياجِ."
The college is "beside the university."	الكُلِّيَّةُ "بِجانِبِ الجامِعَةِ."

The professor is with the dean "before the Arabic language class."

الأستاذُ مَعَ العَميدِ "قَبْلَ دَرْسِ اللُّغَةِ العَرَبِيَّةِ."

A-11. The predicate is a preposition phrase preceding the subject, which is an adjective, common noun, proper noun or possessive.

Examples:

"in the classroom" are students.	"في الصَّفِ" طُلّابٌ.
"in the street" are cars.	"في الشّارِعِ" سَيّاراتٌ.
"on the table" is my book.	"على الطّاوِلَةِ" كِتابي.
"with my sister in the class" is Ahmed.	"مَعَ أُخْتي في الصَّفِّ" أحْمَدُ.
"In the garden" is Layla.	"في الحَديقَةِ" لَيْلى.
"In the broad street" is my house.	"في الشّارِعِ الواسِعِ" بَيْتي.

A-12. The subject is proper, common, pronoun, or adjective, and the predicate is a verb or verbal sentence. **(More details about verb sentences are in section XI)**

Examples:

Angela "does her homework."	آنْجِلَا "تَعْمَلُ واجِبَها ."
The restaurant "serves Egyptian felafel."	المَطْعَمُ "يقَدِّمُ الفَلافِلَ المِصْرِيَّةَ."
He "studies a lot".	هو "يَدْرُسُ كَثِيراً ."
My professor "writes poetry."	أُسْتاذَتِي "تكْتُبُ الشِّعرَ."
The teacher "teaches the Arabic language."	المُدَرِّسُ "يُدَرِّسُ اللُّغَةَ العَرَبِيَّةَ."

Notes:

Test X: Noun Sentence

X-1. Follow the instructions:

- Choose the best combination of subjects and adjective predicates from Columns **1** and **2**.
- Construct meaningful noun sentences.
- Pay attention to the gender forms of the predicates.
- Fill your answer choices in Column **3**.
- *The first row contains a sample answer:*

3 **Noun sentences**	2 **Predicates**	1 **Subjects**
هو عَطْشَانٌ	عَطْشَانٌ thirsty	أخِي
	أخْضَرٌ	البِنتُ
	واسِعٌ	**هو**
	طَيِّبٌ	الشَّجَرَةُ
	مُجْتَهِدٌ	غُرفَتُكَ
	أحْمَرٌ	الشَّارِعُ
	صَغِيرٌ	السَّيَّارَةُ
	عَالِيَةٌ	والدَتِي
	جَوعَانٌ	البَنْكُ Bank
	قَرِيبٌ	البِنَايَةُ

X-2. Read the noun sentences in Column **1**. Identify the subjects and the predicates. Rewrite each in the corresponding Columns **2** and **3**. *The first row contains a sample answer:*

3 Predicates	2 Subjects	1 Noun sentences
سَوداءُ.	القِطَّةُ	القِطَّةُ سَوداءُ.
		كُتُبُنَا في مَكتَبةِ الكُلِّيَّة.
		البِنْتُ تَشْرَبُ الحَلِيب.
		الكِتابُ عَلَىٰ الطَّاوِلَة.
		طَبِيبٌ والِدِي أَمْرِيكِيٌّ.
		أنا أُسْتاذَةٌ عَرَبِيَّةٌ.
		آنْجِلا هِيَ أُسْتاذَةٌ.
		نَحْنُ طُلَّابٌ في صَفِّ التَّأريخ.
		أنتم زُمَلائي.
		هِيَ في بَيْتِها الكَبير.

X-3. Translate the following noun sentences into Arabic:

1. My father is a kind man.

2. The house is enormous.

3. My cat is black.

4. We are students.

5. In the street are cars and houses.

6. The students are Americans.

7. The car is new.

8. I am a student at a college. My college is far away.

9. The teacher is Egyptian.

10. My sister is a hard-working girl.

X-4. Translate the following noun sentences into English:

١. كَلْبُ صَدِيْقِي بُنِّيٌّ . (brown)

٢. الكَلْبُ الأَبْيَضُ في الشَّارِع.

٣. القِطَّةُ بَيضَاءٌ .

٤. مَكْتَبُ المُدِيْرِ في هٰذِهِ البِنَايَة.

٥. غُرْفَتُكُم صَغيرَةٌ.

٦. أُسْرَتُنا كَبيرَةٌ.

٧. والِدَتي مَعَ أخِي.

٨. مَعِي كُتُبٌ كَثِيْرَةٌ.

٩. مكتَبَةُ الكُلِّيَّةِ بَعِيدَةٌ.

١٠. في غُرْفَتِي طَاوِلَةٌ وَكُرْسِيٌّ.

X-5. Choose the best predicates of adjectives, adjective phrases, Idafa and preposition phrases, noun sentences, and verb sentences from Table **1** that are the best choices for the subjects in Table **2**. Rewrite the new sentences in the blanks in Table 2. *The first row contains a sample answer:*

Table (1) Predicates

في الشَّارِعِ	واسِعَةٌ	**في الجَرِيْدَةِ**
جَمِيلٌ وَواسِعٌ	يَقْرَأُ كِتَابَهُ	هِيَ أُسْتَاذَتِي.
طَالِبٌ جَدِيدٌ في صَفِّي	مُدَرِّسَةُ اللُّغَةِ العَرَبِيَّةِ	عَالِيَةٌ في مَدِينَةِ نِيُويُورك
في مَكْتَبَةِ الجَامِعَة	تَكْتُبُ الوَاجِبَ	سُكَّرٌ كُوبِيٌّ

Table (2) Subjects

١. الأخْبَارُ في الجَرِيْدَةِ.
٢. سَامْيَة
٣. بَيْتُكِ
٤. كَرِيْم

٥. السَّيَّارَاتُ
٦. الحَاسُوبُ
٧. الغُرفَةُ
٨. أُخْتِي
٩. وَالِدَتِي
١٠. هٰذا
١١. أحْمَد
١٢. البِنَايَاتُ

X-6. Select a subject from the word bank that best fits each predicate in the list below. Fill in the blanks to complete the sentence. *The first row contains a sample answer:*

المبتدأ   The subject

النَّهارُ	رِيم	كُلِّيَّةُ الأَدَبِ العَرَبِيّ
نَحْنُ	الكُتُبُ	الوَلَدُ الصَّغيرُ
والِدِي	أُسْتاذِي	سَليمٌ
أَساتِذَةُ كُلِّيَّتِنا	الطُّلّابُ	مِصْرُ

الخبر   The Predicate

١. <u>الوَلَدُ الصَّغيرُ شَرِبَ الحَليبَ</u>.

٢. ـــــــــــــــــــــــــ في المَغْرِبِ.

٣. ـــــــــــــــــــــــــ في صَفِّ الأَدَبِ العَرَبِيّ.

٤. ـــــــــــــــــــــــــ مُشْمِسٌ.

٥. ＿＿＿＿＿＿＿＿＿＿ كَاتِبٌ وَ شَاعِرٌ.*

(*writer كَاتِبٌ , poet شَاعِرٌ)

٦. ＿＿＿＿＿＿＿＿＿＿ فِي المَكْتَبَةِ.

٧. ＿＿＿＿＿＿＿＿＿＿ مُوَظَّفٌ كَبِيرٌ.

٨. ＿＿＿＿＿＿＿＿＿＿ في قِسْمِ الكِيمْيَاءِ.

٩. ＿＿＿＿＿＿＿＿＿＿ من البِلادِ الأُورُوبِّيَةِ.

١٠. ＿＿＿＿＿＿＿＿＿＿ مَرْكَزُ الثَّقَافَةِ العَرَبِيَّةِ.

١١. ＿＿＿＿＿＿＿＿＿＿ نَذْهَبُ إِلَى السِّينَمَا.

١٢. ＿＿＿＿＿＿＿＿＿＿ يَدرُسُونَ كَثِيراً.

X-7. Rearrange the order of the following words to construct meaningful sentences:

١. الطَّالِبُ ‒ هَل ‒ عربيٌّ ‒ هٰذا ‒ ؟

٢. دَرْسٌ ‒ هٰذا ‒ اللُّغَةِ ‒ الإبْتِدَائي ‒ العَرَبِيَّة

٣. الفيزياءِ ‒ تُريدُ ‒ لِماذا ‒ كِتابَ ‒ ؟

٤. أنا ‒ القِصَّةَ ‒ أعْرِفُ ‒ لا ‒ هٰذِهِ

٥. كُلِّيَّةٌ ‒ في ‒ بَعيدَةٌ ‒ مَدينَةِ ‒ العُلُومِ ‒ بَغْداد

٦. في ‒ جَديدةٌ ‒ المَكْتَبَةِ ‒ كُتُبٌ

٧. إلىٰ ‒ يَذهَبُون ‒ مَدْرَسَتِهِم ‒ الأوْلادُ

٨. أفْرادُ ‒ التِّلفَاز ‒ الغُرْفَةِ ‒ الأُسْرَةِ ‒ في ‒ يُشَاهِدُونَ

٩. دَرَجَةُ ‒ هُنا ‒ جِداً ‒ عَالِيَةٌ ‒ الصَّيْفِ ‒ الحَرَارَةِ ‒ في

١٠. أحمَدُ ‒ الجَريدَةَ ‒ دائِماً ‒ الصَّباحِ ‒ في ‒ يَقْرَأ

X-8. Translate into English the following story "القِصَّة" about Kareem and Reem:

كَرِيْم طَالِبٌ عَرَبِيٌّ. يَدرُسُ هَنْدَسَةَ الكُمْبْيُوتَر "الحَاسُوب" لِشَهادَةِ الدُّكْتُورَاه في جَامِعَةِ التَّكْنُولُوجْيَا. أُخْتُهُ اُسْمُها رِيْم. هِيَ تَدْرُسُ في الجَامِعَةِ لِشَهادَةِ الماجِسْتِير في التَّرْبِيَة. والدُ كَرِيْم و رِيم اُسْمُهُ أَحْمَد. هو طَبيبٌ. والِدَةُ كَرِيْم و رِيم اُسْمُها لَيْلَىٰ. هي مُدَرِّسَةٌ في جَامِعَةٍ عَرَبِيَّةٍ. كَرِيْم يُرِيدُ العَمَلَ مُدَرِّساً لِعِلْمِ الحَاسُوب . وَ رِيم تُرِيدُ أَن تَعْمَلَ مُدَرِّسَةً في كُلِّيَّةِ التَّرْبِيَّة.

Translation:

X-9. Read the story about Kareem and Reem. Identify an example for each term listed in Column **1,** and write your selection in **Arabic** in Column **2**. *The first row contains a sample answer:*

1	2
one noun sentence جُمْلَة إسْمِيَّة	كَريم طَالِبٌ عَرَبِيٌّ.
one verb sentence جُمْلَة فِعْلِيَّة	
a subject and predicate in a noun sentence مُبْتَدَأ وَخَبَر	
one subject in a noun sentence مُبْتَدَأ في جُمْلَة إسْمِيَّة	
one predicate in a noun sentence خَبَر في جُمْلَة إسْمِيَّة	
one adjective phrase تَعْبِيرُ الصِّفَة	

one Idafa phrase تَعبِيرُ الإضَافَة	
one preposition phrase تَعبِيرُ الجَر	

X-11. Compose a few sentences or phrases about yourself using constructs you learned from the Kareem and Reem story:

X-12. Choose the subjects and predicates from Tables **1** and **2** to form noun sentences that correspond to the images in Table **3**. Write the subject-predicate combination in the blank next to its image. *The first row of Table 3 contains a sample choice:*

Table 1: Subjects

بَيْتُنا في المَدِينَة		الطُّلَّاب والطَّالِبَات
صَدِيقِي أحمَد		سَيَّارَةُ أخِي الجَدِيدَة
والِدِي		الجَوّ في ألاسْكا في الشِّتاء
الأُسْتاذُ		أنا و زُمَلائي
سَمَر		شَمْسُ النَّهارِ

Table 2: Predicates

جَمِيلَةٌ في فلوريدا		في المَكْتَبة
حَمْراء.		مَعَ والِدَتي و أُخْتي
في صَفِّ اللُّغَةِ العَرَبِيَّة		في مَكْتَبِه
بارِدٌ ومُثْلِج		يقرأ كِتاباً عَن الأدَبِ العَرَبي
طالِبَةٌ مُجْتَهِدَة		كَبِيرٌ جِدّاً.

198

Table (3) Images

Notes

Section XI: The Verb Sentence

الجُمْلَة الفِعْلِيَّة

The verb sentence is a combination of related and meaningful word composition about an action ("verb" فِعْل), who is doing the action ("subject" فَاعِل), and who receives the action ("object" مَفْعولٌ بِه.) The following is a description of these three parts of verb sentences.

The Verb "action فِعْل":

A. Types of verbs

The verb in the sentence can be conjugated in the past tense, فِعْلٌ مَاضِي, present tense فِعْلٌ مُضَارِع, future tense فِعْلُ المُسْتَقْبَل, and imperative tense فِعْلُ الأَمْر.

A-1. The past verb فِعْلٌ مَاضِي

In English the word *"wrote"* is a past verb. In Arabic, it also translates in the past tense of كَتَبَ which is the ***start-up that forms different types of the verb/s and its related gender and quantity.*** To simplify the construction of the tenses in the verb sentences we can pre-determined that the "subject" فَاعِل is third person masculine "*he* هو" and feminine "*she* هي."

- The verb كَتَبَ is a past singular masculine verb with **FatHa** on each of the three consonants. With this past form, it is understood that the verb references the third-person masculine subject "هو كَتَبَ."

- For the feminine singular past verb, add the feminine suffix ـتْ at the end of the masculine past verb to create the feminine verb كَتَبَتْ. This verb references the third-person feminine subject "هي كَتَبَتْ".

A-2. Present Verb "he/she writes" فِعْل مُضَارِع

To create this verb tense, start with the past masculine verb:

- Add prefix (يَـ) with **fatHa** to the past verb كَتَبَ
- Replace the **fatHa** on the first letter كَـ with **sukoon** كْـ
- Replace **fatHa** on the second letter ـتَـ with **damma** ـتُـ
- Replace **fatHa** on the third letter ـبَ with **damma** ـبُ
- The present masculine verb is هو يَكْتُبُ
- To form the feminine present verb, add the **prefix letter** (تَـ) with **fatHa** to the masculine past verb كَتَبَ
- Replace the **fatHa** on the first letter كَـ with **sukoon** كْـ
- Replace **fatHa** on the second letter ـتَـ with **damma** ـتُـ
- Replace **fatHa** on the third letter ـبَ with **damma** ـبُ
- The feminine present verb is هي تَكْتُبُ

A-3. Future Verb "he/she will write" فِعْلُ المُسْتَقْبل

To construct the Arabic form, the following are steps to create the masculine and feminine future verbs:

- Start with the masculine present verb. Add the prefix letter س to the verb يَكْتُبُ
- The future verb is هو سَيَكْتُبُ
- OR precede the present verb يَكْتُبُ by the word "will" سَوْفَ
- The masculine future is هو سَوْفَ يَكْتُبُ

204

- To form the feminine future verb, add the prefix letter سَ to the feminine present verb تَـكْـتُـبُ

- The feminine future is هي سَـتَـكْـتُـبُ

- OR هي سَوْفَ تَـكْـتُـبُ

A-4. Imperative Verb "you write" 'm-f': فِعْلُ الأمْر

The Arabic subject for the masculine and feminine Imperative verb is the second person أنتَ or أنتِ. The following are the steps for the imperative verb.

- Start with the past verb كَـتَـبَ

- Add prefix letter أُ with damma to the past verb

- Replace the **fatHa** on the first letter كَـ with **sukoon** كْـ

- Replace **fatHa** on the second letter ـتَـ with **damma** ـتُـ

- Replace **fatHa** on the third letter ـبَ with **sukoon** ـبْ

- The imperative verb for masculine is أُكْتُبْ

- To form the feminine imperative verb, follow the steps to form the masculine imperative verb

- Replace **sukoon** on the fourth letter of the verb ـبْ with **kasra** ـبِ

- Add the suffix letter ـي to the end of the verb

- The feminine imperative verb is أنتِ أُكْتُـبِـي

NOTE: *Future and imperative verbs are not studied further or included in the tests.*
Other details about verbs are included in section XII, "The Arabic verb root system."

Practice writing the following masculine and feminine past and present forms for هو and هي:

سَمِعَ "heard"   شَرِبَ "drank"   ذَهَبَ "went"

B. **Conjugations of the verb** تَصْرِيفُ الفِعْل

The past or present consonant verbs conjugate in a standard form for singular or plural.

B-1. The past verb is singular, the subject is singular:

- The masculine past verb is "studied" دَرَسَ and the subject is "the student" الطَّالِبُ

- The subject is "the student, masculine 3rd person singular" الطَّالِبُ

- The combination of the verb followed by the student is

    دَرَسَ الطَّالِبُ

- The feminine past verb is دَرَسَتْ

    o The subject is "the student, feminine 3rd person singular" الطَّالِبَةُ

    o The combination of the verb followed by its feminine subject is دَرَسَتْ الطَّالِبَةُ

B-2. The present verb is singular, the subject is singular:

- The masculine present verb is "studies" يَدْرُسُ

    o The subject is "the student" الطَّالِبُ.

    o The conjugated present verb is يَدْرُسُ الطَّالِبُ

- The feminine present verb is تَدْرُسُ
    - The subject is "the student" الطَّالِبَةُ
    - The conjugated present verb is تَدْرُسُ الطَّالِبَةُ

B-3. The past verb is singular the subject is 3rd person plural:

- The masculine singular past verb is "studied" دَرَسَ
    - The subject is "the students, masculine 3rd person plural" الطُّلَّابُ.
    - The conjugated past verb is singular دَرَسَ الطُّلَّابُ
- *The* feminine singular past verb is دَرَسَت
    - The subject is "the students, feminine 3rd person plural" الطَّالِبَاتُ

    The conjugated past verb is singular دَرَسَت

    - دَرَسَت الطَّالِبَاتُ

B-4. The present verb is singular the subject is 3rd person plural:

- the students "studies 'm'" يَدْرُسُ الطُّلَّابُ
- the students "studies 'f'" تَدْرُسُ الطَّالِبَاتُ

Practice conjugating the following verbs in bold into masculine and feminine past and present forms for the plural subjects:
(الطُّلَّابُ), (الطَّالِبَاتُ)

ذَهَبَ "went"

شَرِبَ "drank"

سَمِعَ "heard"

B-5. The following table displays the standard conjugation of the verb forms for the personal pronoun subjects.

*The subject gender prefixes and suffixes are in **bold**.*

Examples: The verb " **wrote**" كَتَبَ

فعل مضارع	فعل ماضي	ضَمِير	Pronouns
أكْتُبُ	كَتَبْتُ	أنا	1st person singular
نَكْتُبُ	كَتَبْنَا	نَحْنُ	1st person plural
تَكْتُبُ	كَتَبْتَ	أنتَ	2nd person singular masculine
تَكْتُبِين	كَتَبْتِ	أنتِ	2nd person singular feminine
تَكْتُبُون	كَتَبْتُم	أنتُم	2nd person plural 'm-f,p'
يَكْتُبُ	كَتَبَ	هو	3rd person singular masculine
تَكْتُبُ	كَتَبَتْ	هي	3rd person singular feminine
يَكْتُبُون	كَتَبُوا	هم	3rd person plural 'm-f,p'

(Note) In Arabic grammar:

- **When the verb precedes the plural noun or pronoun subjects it should conjugate into a singular masculine or feminine form.**
- **When the verb follows the plural subject it should conjugate into the plural masculine or feminine form.**
- **The subject gender indicators (markers) in the verb conjugation forms are the attached suffixes.**

C. The Object المَفْعُول بِهِ

المَفْعُول بِهِ is the receiver of the action of the verb. Its function is similar to the English construct of the verb object.

Types of Objects:

C-1. The object is a direct singular 'm,f', or plural 'm-f,p' noun:

It is a definite singular noun with **fatHa** or indefinite with **double fatHa** (tenween alfatHa.) For example البَيتَ or بَيتاً

- It is a direct definite or indefinite masculine plural adjective with the suffix ين. For example المُدَرِّسِين or مُدَرِّسِين
- It is a direct definite or indefinite feminine plural with suffixes اتِ or اتٍ. For example البَنَاتِ or بَنَاتٍ
- It is a direct object of adjective phrases and Idafa phrases
- It is a proposition phrase indirect object of an intransitive verb
- The following table displays the types of objects in a sentence as part of the combination of verb فعل + subject فاعل + object مفعول به
- In Arabic, the subject pronoun may not appear in the sentence. It is referenced as the attached gender suffix

C-2. The following table displays **the verb sentences** with the pronoun as the subject and the object as a definite singular noun "the story" القِصَّةَ or indefinite "a story" قِصَّةً.

Note: *In the following table, the letter suffix that is attached to the verb is its pronoun subject indicator "فاعل" may or may not appear after the verb. Grammatically it is a correct verb construct to attach it only to its subject pronoun suffix. For example,* كَتَبْتُ أنا القِصَّةَ *is correctly re-written as* كَتَبْتُ القِصَّةَ. *The suffix in bold references the subject pronoun* "أنا."

Examples: The verb sentence

فعل مضارع + فاعل + مفعول به	فعل ماضي + فاعل + مفعول به	فعل مضارع	فعل ماضي	فاعل
أَكْتُبُ أنا القِصَّةَ/ قِصَّةً. أو أَكْتُبُ القِصَّةَ/ قِصَّةً.	كَتَبْتُ أنا القِصَّةَ/ قِصَّةً. أو كَتَبْتُ القِصَّةَ/ قِصَّةً.	أَكْتُبُ	كَتَبْتُ	أنا
نَكْتُبُ نَحْنُ القِصَّةَ/ قِصَّةً. نَكْتُبُ القِصَّةَ/ قِصَّةً.	كَتَبْنا نَحْنُ القِصَّةَ/ قِصَّةً. كَتَبْنا القِصَّةَ/ قِصَّةً.	نَكْتُبُ	كَتَبْنا	نَحْنُ
تَكْتُبُ أنتَ القِصَّةَ/ قِصَّةً. تَكْتُبُ القِصَّةَ/ قِصَّةً.	كَتَبْتَ أنتَ القِصَّةَ/ قِصَّةً. كَتَبْتَ القِصَّةَ/ قِصَّةً.	تَكْتُبُ	كَتَبْتَ	أنتَ
تَكْتُبينَ أنتِ القِصَّةَ/ قِصَّةً. تَكْتُبينَ القِصَّةَ/ قِصَّةً.	كَتَبْتِ أنتِ القِصَّةَ/ قِصَّةً. كَتَبْتِ القِصَّةَ/ قِصَّةً.	تَكْتُبينَ	كَتَبْتِ	أنتِ
تَكْتُبونَ أنتُم القِصَّةَ/ قِصَّةً. تَكْتُبونَ القِصَّةَ/ قِصَّةً.	كَتَبْتُم أنتُم القِصَّةَ/ قِصَّةً. كَتَبْتُم القِصَّةَ/ قِصَّةً.	تَكْتُبونَ	كَتَبْتُم	أنتُم
يَكْتُبُ هو القِصَّةَ/ قِصَّةً. يَكْتُبُ القِصَّةَ/ قِصَّةً.	كَتَبَ هو القِصَّةَ/ قِصَّةً. كَتَبَ القِصَّةَ/ قِصَّةً.	يَكْتُبُ	كَتَبَ	هو
تَكْتُبُ هي القِصَّةَ/ قِصَّةً. تَكْتُبُ القِصَّةَ/ قِصَّةً.	كَتَبَتْ هي القِصَّةَ/ قِصَّةً. كَتَبَتْ القِصَّةَ/ قِصَّةً.	تَكْتُبُ	كَتَبَتْ	هي
يَكْتُبونَ هم القِصَّةَ/ قِصَّةً. يَكْتُبونَ القِصَّةَ/ قِصَّةً.	كَتَبوا هم القِصَّةَ/ قِصَّةً. كَتَبوا القِصَّةَ/ قِصَّةً.	يَكْتُبونَ	كَتَبوا	هم

C-3. The object is definite or indefinite masculine or feminine plural adjective:

Past: دَرَّسَ الأسْتاذُ الأمريكِيِّينَ.   دَرَّسَ الأسْتاذُ أمريكِيِّينَ.

دَرَّسَت الأسْتاذَةُ الأمريكِيِّينَ.   دَرَّسَت الأسْتاذَةُ أمريكِيِّينَ.

Present: يُدَرِّسُ الأسْتاذُ الأمريكِيِّينَ.   يُدَرِّسُ الأسْتاذُ أمريكِيِّينَ.

تُدَرِّسُ الأسْتاذَةُ الأمريكِيِّينَ.   تُدَرِّسُ الأسْتاذَةُ أمريكِيِّينَ.

Past: دَرَّسَ الأسْتاذُ الأمريكِيّاتِ.   دَرَّسَ الأسْتاذُ أمريكِيّاتٍ.

دَرَّسَت الأسْتاذَةُ الأمريكِيّاتِ.   دَرَّسَت الأسْتاذَةُ أمريكِيّاتٍ.

Present: يُدَرِّسُ الأسْتاذُ الأمريكِيّاتِ.   يُدَرِّسُ الأسْتاذُ أمريكِيّاتٍ.

تُدَرِّسُ الأسْتاذَةُ الأمريكِيّاتِ.   تُدَرِّسُ الأسْتاذَةُ أمريكِيّاتٍ.

C-4. The object is a definite or indefinite masculine or feminine adjective phrase:

Past: حَفِظَ* أخي الشِّعْرَ** العَرَبِيَّ.   أو حفِظَ أخِي شِعْراً عَرَبِيّاً.

حَفِظَت* أُختي الشِّعْرَ** العَرَبِيَّ.   أو حفِظَت أُختي شِعْراً عَرَبِيّاً.

Present: يَحْفَظُ أخي الشِّعْرَ العَرَبِيَّ.   أو يَحْفَظُ أخِي شِعْراً عَرَبِيّاً.

تَحْفَظُ أُختِي الشِّعْرَ العَرَبِيَّ.   أو تَحْفَظُ أُختِي شِعْراً عَرَبِيّاً.

(*) memorized (**) poem

Past: أكَلَت والِدَتي الفَلافِلَ المِصرِيَّة.   أو أكَلَت والِدَتي فَلافِلاً مِصرِيَّةً.

Present: تأكُلُ والِدَتي الفَلافِلَ المِصرِيَّة.   أو تأكُلُ والِدَتي فَلافِلاً مِصرِيَّةً.

C-5. The object is Idafa phrase:

Past: عَمِلَ زَميلي واجِبَ اللُّغَةِ العَرَبِيَّة.

عَمِلَت زَميلَتي واجِبَ اللُّغَةِ العَرَبِيَّة.

Present: يَعْمَلُ زَمِيلي واجِبَ اللُّغَةِ العَرَبِيَّةِ.

تَعْمَلُ زَمِيلَتي واجِبَ اللُّغَةِ العَرَبِيَّةِ.

C-6. The object is indirect definite or indefinite preposition phrase:

ذَهَبَ كَرِيم إلى مُخْتَبَرِ الحاسُوبِ في الجامِعةِ.

تُدَرِّسُ والِدَتي في مَدْرَسَةٍ إِبْتِدائِيَّةٍ بَعِيْدَةٍ.

D. Grammatical position of the verb sentence:

- When the verb or verb sentence follows a singular, plural noun or pronoun subject, the verb or the verb sentence forms the predicate خَبَر to the subject مُبْتَدَأ. The verb then must agree in gender and number with the subject. This new sentence becomes a noun sentence.

  Examples: *(Noun Sentence)*

    o The subject is singular masculine الطّالِبُ the verb conjugates in the singular masculine

    الطّالِبُ دَرَسَ الدَّرْسَ.   الطّالِبُ يَدْرُسُ الدَّرْسَ.

    o The subject is singular feminine الطّالِبَةُ the verb conjugates in the singular feminine

    الطّالِبَةُ دَرَسَتِ الدَّرْسَ.   الطّالِبَةُ تَدْرُسُ الدَّرْسَ.

    o The subject is masculine and feminine plural الطّالِباتُ ، الطّلّابُ
    o The verb conjugates in the plural

    الطّلّابُ و الطّالِباتُ دَرَسوا الدَّرْسَ.

    الطّلّابُ و الطّالِباتُ يَدْرُسونَ الدَّرْسَ.

- When the verb in the same sentence above precedes the plural masculine or feminine subject, the verb conjugates in the singular form and the sentence becomes a verb sentence. This change in the construct does not have any effect on the original meaning of the sentence.

  Examples: (Verb Sentence)

  دَرَسَ الطُّلَّابُ الدَّرْسَ. يَدْرُسُ الطُّلَّابُ الدَّرْسَ.

  دَرَسَتِ الطَّالِبَاتُ الدَّرْسَ. تَدْرُسُ الطَّالِبَاتُ الدَّرْسَ.

Notes

Test XI: Verb Sentences

XI-1. Translate into Arabic the following verb sentences. Make sure to follow the gender and quantity indicated in quotes. *The first sentence is a sample translation.*

1. Wrote her homework. 'fs'   ١. كَتَبَت "هِيَ" واجِبَها.

2. Works in an Arab country. 'ms'

3. Studies in America. 'fs'

4. What did Mona study? 'fs'

5. Read many books. 'past mp'

6. Play basketball in the college. 'present m-f,p'

7. Teaches in an Arab College. 'present fs'

8. Want to drink tea? '1st person mp'

9. Lives with her family. 'fs'

10. Go to the school. 'present m-f,p'

XI-2. Translate into Arabic the following noun sentences with the verb sentence as the predicate. *First sentence 1 is a sample translation:*

1. Rana wrote a letter to her mother. ١. رَنا كَتَبَت رِسالةً إلىٰ أُمِّهَا.

2. I teach the Arabic Language and Culture.

3. My friend Ali goes to college every day.

4. My English professor is American 'fs.'

5. My sister writes good stories.

6. I studied the Arabic and French languages in my school.

7. She went to the university with my brother.

8. My father works at the school.

9. My colleagues drink coffee in the cafeteria.

10. Mariam watches (تُشَاهِد) the Arabic language video with her mother.

XI-3. Read the following instructions then write your answer choices:
- Identify each verb sentence or noun sentence.
- Change each verb sentence into a noun sentence or a noun sentence into a verb sentence.
- Use independent pronouns (I, we; you "fs," "ms"; you "fp," "mp"; he, she, (they, 'f-m, p') as subjects when needed.
- *The first sentence contains a sample answer:*

١. تَدْرُسُ سُونيا اللُّغَةَ العربيَّة.   *'verb sentence'*
   سُونيا تَدْرُسُ اللُّغَةَ العربيَّة.   *'noun sentence'*

٢. جُون وكَرِيْم ومَايْكِل يَدْرُسُون اللُّغَة والثَّقَافة العَرَبِيَّة.

٣. أَخَذَ سَعِيْد وشَرِيْف وأحْمَد الكُتُبَ إلىٰ المَكْتَبة.

٤. هم يَكتبُون رِسالةً إلىٰ والِدَتِهِم.

٥. تَسْكُن رِيْم مع لَيلىٰ وصديقَتِها في بَيت قَريب من الكُلِّيَّة.

٦. سليم يَدرُس لِشَهادَةِ الدُّكْتُوراه.

٧. أدرُسُ في كُلِّيَّةٍ مَشْهُورَةٍ "famous".

٨. نَبيلُ يَكْتُبُ واجِبَهُ كُلَّ يَوْمٍ.

٩. أُحِبُّ الصَّيْفَ في مَدينةِ بَيْروت اللُّبنانِيَّة.

١٠. نَلْعَبُ كُرَةَ السَّلَّةِ في فَصْلِ الرَّبيع كُلَّ أُسْبُوع.

١١. أَعْرِفُ كُلَّ زُمَلائي في صَفِّ اللُّغَةِ الإسْبَانِيَّة.

١٢. أولادُ عَمّي يَعْمَلُونَ في شَرِكَةِ "company" والِدِهِم.

١٣. المُهَنْدِسُون يَعْمَلُونَ في المَكْتَبِ كَثيراً.

١٤. الطُّلَّابُ يَكْتُبُونَ دُرُوسَهُم.

١٥. أحْمَد وَمُحَمَّد وَعَلّي يَدْ رُسُونَ في مَرْكَزِ التَّكْنُلُوجْيَا.

XI-4. Answer the following with your choices:

- Select from the word bank the past or present verb that best fills in the blanks.
- Conjugate the verbs to agree with the subjects. (All verbs are 3rd person singular.)
- Use each verb only once.
- *Sentence number 1 contains an underlined sample answer:*

read قَرَأَ ت	drank شَرِبَ	lives تَسْكُنُ	wanted أَرَادَ
goes out يَخَرُجُ	watched شَاهَدَ	worked **عَمِلَتْ**	likes يُحِبُّ
eats تَأْكُلُ	received حَصَلَ	writes يَكْتُبُ	went ذَهَبَ

١. هي **عَمِلَتْ** وَاجِبَها.

٢. الطُّلَّابُ _____ مِنَ الكُلِّيَّة.

٣. أُخْتِي _____ مع والِدِي ووالِدَتِي وأخِي الصَّغير.

٤. _____ الطَّالِباتُ عَلىٰ شَهاداتٍ عَالِيَةٍ في اللُّغَات.

٥. نَحْنُ _____ التَّلفَازَ يَومَ الجُمْعَة.

٦. هو _____ الحَليبَ في الصَّباح.

٧. ماذا _____ يَا لَمْياء ؟

٨. هل _____ الكِتابَ؟

٩. هم _____ إلىٰ المَكْتَبة.

١٠. أخي _____ الذِهابَ إلىٰ السِّينَما.

١١. صَديقي مَازِن _____ واجِبَ اللُّغةِ العَرَبيَّة.

١٢. لَيْلىٰ _____ قَلِيلاً في الصَّباح.

XI-5. Read the instructions to help you with your answer choices:

- List **A** is an English noun and verb sentences
- List **B** is a group of separate Arabic words.
- Rearrange the words in list **B** to create new noun or verb sentences.
- Write in List **C** the new sentences that best match the meaning of each English sentence in List **A**
- *The first entry in the lists **A** and **C** is a sample answer:*

List A - English noun and verb sentences:

1. <u>*Is the temperature degree high in the summer?*</u>
2. Ahmed went to Arizona State.
3. I wrote my friend an Arabic language letter.
4. My friends and I love tea.
5. I Like delicious Arabic food and Felafel with bread.
6. He works with his colleague in the library.
7. He lives in a house close to the college.
8. I study with my classmates in the evening.
9. Have a difficult exam in the morning.
10. Is Laila reading the chemistry book?

List B - Group of Arabic words:

١. الحَرَارَةِ ـ دَرَجَةٌ ـ الصَّيْف ـ هَل ـ في ـ عَالِيَة؟

٢. أحْمَد ـ وِلَايَةِ ـ إلىٰ ـ ذَهَبَ ـ أريزونا

٣. كَتَبْتُ ـ العَرَبِيَّةِ ـ رِسَالَةً ـ صَدِيقي ـ بِاللُّغَةِ ـ إلىٰ

٤. نُحِبُّ ـ وَ ـ الشَّايَ ـ أنا ـ أصْدِقائي

٥. و ـ الأكلَ ـ أُحِبُّ ـ العَرَبِيَ ـ الخُبز ـ الفَلافِل ـ مع ـ الطَّيِّب

٦. عَمِلَ ـ مَعَ ـ فِي ـ زَميلِه ـ المَكْتَبَة

٧. بَيْت ـ مِن ـ يَسْكُن ـ الكُلِّيَّة ـ في ـ قَرِيْب

٨. في ـ مَعَ ـ أدْرُسُ ـ المَسَاء ـ زَمِيلِي

٩. الصَّباح ـ صَعْباً ـ في ـ إمْتِحاناً ـ عِنْدِي

١٠. تَقْرأ ـ هل ـ لَيْلَىٰ ـ الكِيمْيَاء ـ كِتابَ؟

List C - New rearranged Arabic sentences:

١. <u>هَل دَرَجَةُ الحَرَارَة عَالِيَةٌ في الصَّفِ؟</u>

٢.

٣.

٤.

٥.

٦.

٧.

٨.

٩.

١٠.

XI-6 Conjugate the present verbs into 3rd person feminine and masculine past tense. *The first row contains a sample answer:*

Present verbs	Past Tense المَاضِي		
	Singular Feminine	Singular Masculine	Plural Feminine and Masculine
يَتْرُكُ leaves	تَرَكَت	تَرَكَ	تَرَكُوا
يَنامُ sleeps			
يَأْخُذُ takes			
يَعْلَمُ knows			
يُسَافِرُ travels			
يَركُضُ runs			
يُسَاعِدُ helps			
يَسْبَحُ swims			
يَمْنَعُ prevents			
يَذْهَبُ goes			

XI-7. Conjugate the past verbs into 3rd person feminine and masculine present tense.
The first row contains a sample answer:

Past verbs	Singular feminine	Singular Masculine	Plural Feminine and Masculine
Present Tense المُضَارِع			
spoke تَكَلَّمَ	تَتَكَلَّمُ	يَتَكَلَّمُ	يَتَكَلَّمُون
ate أَكَلَ			
drank شَرِبَ			
heard سَمِعَ			
opened فَتَحَ			
thanked شَكَرَ			
won رَبِحَ			
graduated تَخَرَّجَ			
learned تَعَلَّمَ			
ran away هَرَبَ			

XI-8. Conjugate the verbs in brackets into the **present tense** that best fits in the blanks. *The first conjugation of the verb in bold is a sample answer:*

١. أصْدِقائي **يَذْهَبُونَ** إلىٰ السِّينَمَا.   (ذَهَبَ)

٢. أسَاتِذَةُ اللُّغَةِ _____ العَرَبِيَّة والفِرَنسِيَّة.   (دَرَّسَ)

٣. _____ الطُّلَّابُ إلىٰ المُحاضَرَةِ عن الفَلَك. 'Astronomy'   (إسْتَمَعَ)

٤. العُمَّالُ _____ الغَداءَ.   (أكَلَ)

٥. _____ البناتُ في بيتِ الطَّالِبَاتِ.   (سَكَنَ)

٦. هل _____ أحمد القَهْوَةَ مع السُّكَّرِ؟   (شَرِبَ)

٧. مَن _____ في ترجَمَةِ هٰذِهِ القِصَّة؟   (عَمِلَ)

٨. _____ المُدَرِّسُون والمُدَرِّسَات كُلَّ العُلُومِ في جامِعَتي.   (دَرَّسَ)

٩. هل أنتم _____ الواجِبَ؟   (كَتَبَ)

١٠. هو _____ فيلماً جميلاً في السِّينَمَا.   (شَاهَدَ)

XI-9. Follow the instructions to create **10** meaningful verb sentences:

1. Select the verbs and appropriate subjects and objects from Table **1** to compose the verb sentences. Pay attention to gender and quantity forms.
2. Write the sentences in Table **2** Column **A**.
3. Change those sentences into new noun sentences. Re-write the noun sentences in Column **B**
4. *Columns **A** and **B** in **Table 2** contain a sample answer.*

Table 1

Objects	Subjects	Verbs
صَباحاً	سَلِيْم	يَعْمَلُ
مَسَاءً	صَدِيقَتِي	يَدْرُسُ
دَائِماً	وإخْوَتِي	يَكْتُبُ
كَثِيراً	**المُدَرِّسُ**	يَأْخُذُ
كُتُبَهُ	الطَّالِبُ	يَدْرُسُ
الشَّجَرَة	والِدِي	يَأْكُلُ
الأَدَبَ العَرَبِيَّ	هُم	يَقْرأ
الطَّعَامَ العَرَبِيَّ	نَحْنُ	يُشَاهِدُ
الدَّرْسَ	كَرِيْم	يَأْكُلُ
الواجِباتِ	والِدَتِي	**يُدَرِّسُ**
العَشَاء	أَخِي وأُخْتِي	يَلْعَبُ
فِيلْماً	أَحْمَد	يَزْرَعُ plants
قِصَصاً مُفِيدَةً	أنا	يُسَاعِدُ helps

225

Table 2

A	B
Verb sentences	**Noun sentences**
يُدَرِّسُ المُدَرِّسُ الدَّرسَ	المُدَرِّسُ يُدَرِّسُ الدَّرسَ
1.	
2.	
3.	
4.	
5.	
6.	
7.	
8.	
9.	
10.	

XI-10. Compose Arabic verb sentences (verb + subject + object) about the people in the pictures. Write your sentences next to the corresponding images:

1.

2.

3.

4.

5.

6.

7.

8.

XI-11. Read the following story. Underline the verbs, their subjects, and their objects. Under the lines, label each verb with **"V"**, each subject with **"S"**, and each object with **"O."**:

The Story:

دَرَسَ سَمِيْر في جامِعَة الأدَب في أمْرِيكا. وَحَصَّلَ على شَـهادَةِ الماجْسْتير فِي الأدَبِ الإنْجِلِيزي. يُتَرْجِمُ سَمِيْر قِصَصاً تأرِيخِيَّة كَثِيرَةً مِنَ العَرَبِيَّةِ إِلىٰ الإنْجِلِيزِيَّة. رَجِعَ سَمِيْر إلى بَلَدِهِ العَرَبيّ وهو الآن يُدَرِّسُ اللُّغَةَ الإنْجِلِيزِيَّة في كُلِّيَةِ التَّكْنَلُوجْيَا و يُدَرِّسُ أيضاً الأدَبَ الإنْجِلِيزيّ في مَدْرَسةٍ ثَانَوِيَّةٍ.

أُخْتُ سَمِيْر أُسْمُهَا مَرْيَم. دَرَسَت عِلْمَ الإجْتِماع في كُلِّيَةِ الثَّقَافَة. وتَخَرَّجَت قَبْلَ سَنة. هِيَ الآن تَدْرُسُ هٰذا العِلمَ لِشـهادَةِ الدُّكْتُوراه في جامِعَةٍ أمريكِيَّةٍ. وبَعْدَ الدُّكْتُوراه ، تُريدُ مَرْيَم العَمَلَ في بَلَدٍ عَرَبِيّ.

XI-12. Translate the story in **XI-11** from Arabic to English:

XI-13. Choose one of the following topics to write a 5–6 sentence story in Arabic using yourself as the main character. Use the grammatical constructs and the vocabulary you learned. Also, consult the vocabulary appendices to help your creative writing in Arabic:

- An Arabic class with your classmate
- A meeting with your advisor
- Why do you study Arabic?
- Any other topic about yourself

Notes:

Section XII: Base letters and Patterns

الجُذُور وَالأَوْزَان
Morphological Scale in the Arabic Derivation System
مِيزَان الصَّرف فِي نِظَام الإشْتِقَاق

Most of the words in the Arabic language are derived from standard base letter roots that consist of three consonants. It is a system that the Arabic Language uses to form many verbs and to derive many nouns, including adjective-noun (إسْـمُ الصِّفَة) and Infinitive, verbal noun (المَصْدَر.) In this section, the derivation system covers verb patterns only.

The standard three-base letters template (ف-ع-ل) are the three base consonants of the root system. When connected it reads فْعْل, which means "to do, to act or to perform an activity." When adding vowels to each base letter, for example, **FatHa** it becomes "past tense did" and reads فَعَلَ. When adding a letter, for example, (ا) within the base letter root, it becomes " a subject or an adjective, which is the entity who is doing the activity" and it reads فَاعِلٌ.

The root system is remarkable in its application to provide the students of the Arabic language with ways to enhance their creativity in writing, reading, and conversation.

The following are examples of the base root system and how to use it. The translations of these examples are comparable meanings in English.

Examples:

- فْعْل may change into فَعَلَ by changing the **sukoon** on each letter to a **fatHa**, which creates the past verb "did."
- For another form of the past tense verb, add **shadda + fatHa** to the past verb فَعَلَ to create فَـعَّـلَ, "enabled to be done or causing someone to do."

- Add a prefix letter (يَـ) to فْعْلْ and replace the **sukoon** on ـعْـ and ـلْ with **fatHa** and **damma** to create the form of the present tense, يَفْعَلُ "does."

- Add infix letter (ا) and suffixes (ون) to فْعْلْ and replace the **sukoon** on ـعْـ with kasra to create the plural adjective فَاعِلُون "doers."

- **A change of vowels and letters creates new verbs, but the base three-letter root remains the basic part of the new word.**

  1. **Structure of Verb Patterns**

The verbs formed from each three-letter base root follow mostly 10 basic patterns. These patterns reference the Roman numerals **I-X**. To create these ten verb patterns, change or add new vowels and letters to the three-letter base ف ـ ع ـ ل. The following are the most common vowels and letters added to the three-letter base of different patterns:

    The vowels are   " FatHa, Kasra, Damma"

    The letters are   س، ت، ل، م، ن، ا، و، ي

Tables (A-C) contain verb patterns I-X. Table (D) contains singular 3rd person masculine past and present verb samples that follow those patterns. English translations of the samples are comparable in meanings to English when applicable:

Table (A) Basic three-letter pattern

Pattern #I

Base Pattern #I	past verb	فَعُلَ or فَعِلَ or فَعَلَ
Base Pattern #I	present verb	يَفْعُلُ or يَفْعِلُ or يَفْعَلُ

236

Table (B) Increased basic pattern with vowels

Pattern #II: Add the vowels Shadda-FatHa and Shadda-Kasra to Pattern #1.

Pattern #II	past verb	فَعَّلَ
Pattern #II	present verb	يُفَعِّلُ

Table (C) Increased basic patterns with vowels and letters

Patterns III through X are formed by adding vowels and letters to the base pattern #I.

Pattern #III	past verb	فَاعَلَ
Pattern #III	present verb	يُفَاعِلُ

Pattern #IV	past verb	أَفْعَلَ
Pattern #IV	present verb	يُفْعِلُ

Pattern #V	past verb	تَفَعَّلَ
Pattern #V	present verb	يَتَفَعَّلُ

Pattern #VI	past verb	تَفَاعَلَ
Pattern #VI	present verb	يَتَفَاعَلُ

Pattern #VII	past verb	إنْفَعَلَ
Pattern #VII	present verb	يَنفَعِلُ

Pattern #VIII	past verb	إفْتَعَلَ
Pattern #VIII	present verb	يَفْتَعِلُ

Pattern #IX	past verb	اِفْعَلَّ
Pattern #IX	present verb	يَفْعَلُّ

Pattern #X	past verb	إِسْتَفْعَلَ
Pattern #X	present verb	يَسْتَفْعِلُ

Table (D) Samples of selected verbs that follow patterns I-X

Base pattern #I, past	Base pattern #I, present
praised or commended "فَعَلَ" مَدَحَ	praises or commends "يَفْعَلُ" يَمْدَحُ
thought or calculated "فَعِلَ" حَسِبَ	thinks or calculates "يَفْعِلُ" يَحْسِبُ
became better "فَعُلَ" حَسُنَ	becomes better "يَفْعُلُ" يَحْسُنُ

Pattern II Shadda added to the 2nd base-letter past فَعَّلَ present يُفَعِّلُ	
دَرَّسَ taught	يُدَرِّسُ teaches
رَحَّبَ welcomed	يُرَحِّبُ welcomes
فَكَّرَ thought	يُفَكِّرُ thinks

Pattern III

Infix (l) after the 1st base-letter

Past فَاعَلَ | present يُفَاعِلُ

شَهَدَ / شَاهَدَ watched/witnessed	يشْهَدُ / يُشَاهِدُ watches / witnesses
قَبِلَ / قَابَلَ met/accepted	يَقبَلُ / يُقَابِلُ meets/accepts
قَرُبَ / قَارَبَ drew near/ became close	يَقْرُبُ / يُقَارِبُ draws near/ becomes close

Pattern IV

Prefix (l) before the 1st base-letter

past أَفْعَلَ | present يُفْعِلُ

رَسَلَ / أَرْسَلَ sent	يَرْسِلُ / يُرْسِلُ sends
ثَبَتَ / أَثْبَتَ proved/stood firm	يَثْبُتُ / يُثْبِتُ proves/stands firm
خَرَجَ / أَخْرَجَ brought out/went out	يَخْرُجُ / يُخْرِجُ brings out/goes out

Pattern V

Prefix (تَـ) the 1st base-letter, Shadda on 2nd base-letter

past تَفَعَّلَ — present يَتَفَعَّلُ

past	present
خَرَّجَ / تَخَرَّجَ graduated/went out	يُخَرِّجُ / يَتَخَرَّجُ graduates/goes out
عَلَّمَ / تَعَلَّمَ learned from/learned	يُعَلِّمُ / يَتَعَلَّمُ learns from/learns
حَدَّثَ/تَحَدَّثَ conversed with/ happened	يُحَدِّثُ / يَتَحَدَّثُ converses /happens

Pattern VI

Prefix (تَـ) the 1st base-letter, infix (ا) before the 2nd base-letter

past تَفَاعَلَ — present يَتَفَاعَلُ

past	present
سَهَّلَ/تَسَاهَلَ became lenient / became easy	يُسَهِّلُ/يَتَسَاهَلُ becomes lenient/becomes easy
نَاقَشَ/تَنَاقَشَ debated with/engraved	يُنَاقِشُ / يَتَنَاقَشُ debates with/engraves
بَدَّلَ/ تَبَادَلَ exchanged/replaced	يُبَدِّلُ / يَتَبَادَلُ exchanges/replaces

Pattern VII
Prefix (إ) and (نْ) onto the 1st base-letter
past إنْفَعَلَ   present يَنْفَعِلُ

إنْقَلَبَ /قَلَبَ turned over/rolled over	يَنْقَلِبُ /يَقْلِبُ turns over/rolls over
إنْقَطَعَ /قَطَعَ severed/cut	يَنْقَطِعُ /يَقْطَعُ severs/cuts
إنْكَسَرَ /كَسَرَ broke into pieces/broke	يَنْكَسِرُ /يَكْسِرُ breaks into pieces/breaks

Pattern VIII
Prefix (إ) the 1st base-letter, infix (تَ) before the 2nd base-letter
Past إفْتَعَلَ   Present يَفْتَعِلُ

إمْتَنَعَ /مَنَعَ refused/prohibited	يَمْتَنِعُ /يَمْنَعُ refuses/prohibits
إقْتَرَبَ /قَرُبَ approached/came closer	يَقْتَرِبُ /يَقْرُبُ approaches/come closer
إرْتَفَعَ /رَفَعَ elevated/pushed up	يَرْتَفِعُ /يَرْفَعُ elevates/pushes up

Pattern IX
Prefix (إ) the 1st base-letter, shadda fatHa on the 3rd base-letter
past إفْعَلَّ   **present** يَفْعَلُّ

past	present
إبْيَضَّ / بَيَضَ became whiter / made it white	يَبْيَضُّ / يَبْيَضُ becomes whiter/whitens
إخْضَرَّ / خَضَرَ became greener/became green	يَخْضَرُّ / يَخْضَرُ becomes greener/becomes green
إسْوَدَّ / سَوَدَ became black/blackened	يَسْوَدُّ / يَسْوَدُ blackens/prevails

Pattern X
Prefix (إ، سـ، تَـ) the 1st three base-letters
past إسْتَفْعَلَ   **present** يَسْتَفْعِلُ

past	present
إسْتَخْدَمَ / خَدَمَ employed/served	يَسْتَخْدِمُ / يَخْدِمُ employs/serves
إسْتَفْهَمَ / فَهِمَ questioned / understood	يَسْتَفْهِمُ / يَفْهَمُ questions/understands
إسْتَقْبَلَ / قَبِلَ received "a guest"/accepted	يَسْتَقْبِلُ / يَقْبَلُ receives "a guest"/accepts

2. Steps to Locate the Three-Letter Base Root in each Verb

Knowing the roots and patterns of Arabic verbs is a helpful tool for mastering new vocabulary and searching for words when using an Arabic-English dictionary. The Hans Wehr Dictionary of Modern Written Arabic, edited by J.M. Cowan, is the most comprehensive resource that derives different lists of verbs and other words by their 3-letter root and relevant patterns.

The following are steps to recognize a verb's three-letter base roots:

1) Determine its pattern by matching the verb with one of the patterns you learned in **Tables A, B, and C.**

2) The verb, 'met' قَابَلَ, for example, corresponds with the standard verb pattern #III (فَاعَلَ.) The vowel sounds are the same, but the consonant sounds are not.

3) Since the three-letter root for فَاعَلَ is ف ـ ع ـ ل, the letter "I" is not part of the root; it is an infix added to the three-letter base that makes pattern #III. Eliminate this infix letter to get the three-letter root ف ـ ع ـ ل.

4) Similarly, the base three-letter root of قَابَلَ should be ق ـ ب ـ ل because the letter "I" in قَابَلَ is an added infix. Eliminate this letter to get to the three-letter root ق - ب - ل.

5) ***The steps of eliminating letters to determine the three-letter base root is the same for any three-consonant verbs. Using this process helps in searching for new vocabulary which ultimately leads to the composition of grammatically correct noun and verb sentences for creative writing.***

3. Application of the verb derivation system in sentences:

verb	pattern number	noun sentence with a past verb *	present verb sentence *
دَرَسَ studied	I	سَمَر **دَرَسَت** الْلُغَةَ العَرَبِيَّة في مِصْر.	**تَدْرُسُ** سَمَرُ الْلُغَةَ العَرَبِيَّة في مِصْر.
رَحَّبَ welcomed	II	والِدَةُ عَلِيّ **رَحَّبَت** بِصَدِيقِه مايْكِل.	**يُرَحِّبُ** عَلِيّ بِزِيارَةِ والِدَتِه كَثيراً.
شَهِدَ watched	III	أنا وإخوَتي **شاهَدْنا** فيلماً جَيِّداً في السِّينَما.	**نُشاهِدُ** اليَوْمَ فيديو عن فيروسِ الكرونا.
رَسَلَ sent	IV	أنا **أرْسَلْتُ** رَسائِلي في البَريد المُصَدَّق.	**يُرْسِلُ** سَمير واجِبَه إلى الأستاذِ كُلَّ يوم.
خَرَجَ went	V	الإخوةُ سَمير و ريم وأميْر **تَخَرَّجُوا** من الجامِعَة.	**يَتَخَرَّجُ** حَسَن مِنَ المدرَسةِ الثانَوِيَّة بَعْدَ سَنَة.
سَهَّلَ made easy	VI	الحاكِمُ **تَساهَل** في حُكْمِه.	**يَتَساهَلُ** المدَرِّسُ مَعَ طالِبِه المَريض.
سَحَبَ pulled away	VII	فَريقُ كُرةِ القَدَم **إنْسَحَب** مِنَ السِّباق.	**تَنْسَحِبُ** ريم مِنَ المُناظَرة مَساءً.
قَرَّبَ came closer	VIII	كَريْم **إفْتَرَب** من نِهايَةِ الهَدَف.	**نَقْتَرِبُ** أنا وأُخْتي مِنَ الوصولِ إلى بَيتِنا.
خَضَرَ accepted	IX	الشَجَرَةُ **إخْضَرَّت** في الربيع.	**تَخْضَرُّ** أوراقُ الأشجارِ بَعْدَ فَصْلِ الشِّتاء.
قَبِلَ accepted	X	والِدَتي **إسْتَقْبَلَت** صاحِباتِها يَومَ الخَميس.	

244

***New verb vocabulary comparable to English translation:**

welcomed	رَحَّبَت
welcomes	يُرَحِّبُ
visit	بِزِيَارَة
we watched	شاهَدْنَا
good movie	فيْلماً جَيّداً
we watch	نُشَاهِدُ
Coronavirus	فيروس الكرونا
sent or mailed	أرْسَلْتُ
my letters	رَسَائِلي
post office mail	في البَريد

certified mail	في البَريد المُصَدَّق
sends	**يُرْسِلُ**
every day	كُلَّ يَومٍ
they graduated	**تَخَرَّجُوا**
graduates	**يَتَخَرَّجُ**
high school	المدرَسَة الثَّانَوِيَّة
after	بَعْدَ
a year	سَنَة
was lenient	**تَسَاهَلَ**
the judge	الحاكِمُ
his verdict	في حُكْمِهِ

يَتَساهَلُ	is lenient to treat, is easy
المَريض	the sick
إنْسَحَبَت	withdrew
فَريقُ كُرَةِ القَدَم	soccer team
المُبَاراة/سِباق	the game/race
تَنْسَحِبُ رِيْم	Reem withdraws
المُنَاظَرة	debate
مَساءً	in the evening
إقْتَرَبَ	came close
نِهَايَة	end
الهَدَف	the goal

are coming close	نَقْتَرِبُ
from	مِن
arriving	الوُصُول
became green	إخْضَّرَّت
In the spring	في الرَّبيع
becomes green	تَخْضَّرُ
after	بَعْدَ
season	فَصْل
the winter	الشِّتَاء
received	إسْتَقْبَلَت
her friends	صَاحِبَاتِها

all/every	كُلّ
day	يَومَ
Thursday	الخَمِيس
receives	يَسْتَقْبِلُ
the guests	الضُّيوفَ

Notes:

Test XII: Verb base letters and patterns

XII-1. Apply the patterns to the given three-letter base verb roots to build past and present verbs. Consult an Arabic-English dictionary to identify their meanings. Practice reading the newly created verbs:

Pattern #	Patterns	The three-letter base verb root	Past verb	Present verb
I	فَعَلَ / يَفْعَلُ	ق ـ ر ـ أ		
II	فَعَّلَ / يُفَعِّلُ	د ـ ر ـ س		
III	فَاعَلَ / يُفَاعِلُ	ع ـ م ـ ل		
IV	أَفْعَلَ / يُفْعِلُ	ق ـ د ـ م		
V	تَفَعَّلَ / يَتَفَعَّلُ	قَ ـ ر ـ ب		
VI	تَفَاعَلَ / يَتَفَاعَلُ	ع ـ ر ـ ف		
VII	إنْفَعَلَ / يَنفَعِلُ	ق ـ س ـ م		
VIII	إفْتَعَلَ / يَفْتَعِلُ	س ـ م ـ ع		
IX	إفْعَلَّ / يَفْعَلُّ	س ـ و ـ د		
X	إسْتَفْعَلَ / يَسْتَفْعِلُ	م ـ ت ـ ع غ ـ ر ـ ب		

XII-2. Determine the three-letter base roots of the verbs in the table. Write the New roots and their pattern numbers (**Column 3.**)

The first row contains a sample answer:

(1) English	(2) Arabic	(3) 3-base letter root
invested	إِسْتَثْمَر	ث - م - ر "X"
studied	دَرَسَ	
listened	إِسْتَمَعَ	
taught	دَرَّسَ	
treated	عَامَلَ	
broke	إِنْكَسَرَ	
helped	سَاعَدَ	
advanced	تَقَدَّمَ	
pondered	فَكَّرَ	
depended on	إِعْتَمَدَ	

XII-3. Read each verb sentence. Fill in the blanks with your answer choices:
- Write the verb in the verb column
- Determine the verb pattern
- Write it in its column
- *The first raw contains a sample answer:*

Pattern and #	Verb	Sentences
Pattern #II / فَعَّل	دَرَّسَ	١ـ دَرَّسَ أحْمد كِتابَ الفِيزْياء.
		٢ـ عَامَلَ المُدِير المُوَظَّفَ طَيِّباً.
		٣ـ يَسْتَمِعُ سَلِيْم إلى الأخْبار.
		٤ـ نُورا إسْتَمْتَعَت بِالقِصَّة.
		٥ـ إخْضَرَّت الأشْجارُ في فَصْلِ الرَّبيع.
		٦ـ نَجَحَ الطُّلَّابُ في الإمْتِحان النِّهائي.
		٧ـ إكْتَشَفَ الطَّبيبُ دَواءً جَيِّداً.
		٨ـ تَقَدَّمَت لَيْلى في دُروسِها.
		٩ـ تَكَلَّمَ كَريم مَعَ صَديقِه بالهاتِف.
		١٠ـ يَتَراسَلُ الوالِدُ مَعَ وَلَدِهِ كُلَّ يَوم.

XII-4. Choose the derived verb that best fits in the blanks.

The first row contains a sample answer:

Pattern number	Basic Pattern #I	Derived verb
II	عَبَرَ	عَبَّرَ
III	قَطَعَ	
IV	كَسَرَ	
V	رَكَضَ	
VI	قِبلَ	
VII	كَتَبَ	
VIII	فَتَحَ	
IX	خَضُرَ	
X	عَلِمَ	

XII-5. Underline the verb in each sentence. Then fill in the blank with its three-letter base root. Consult the tables of patterns if needed.

First sentence is a sample answer:

١- <u>أَجْتَهِدُ</u> في دَرْسِ اللُّغَةِ العَرَبِيَّةِ لِأَنَّهُ مُفِيدٌ. ج ـ هـ ـ د

٢- نَدْرُسُ الحَاسُوبَ في كُلِّيَّتِنا. _____

٣- قَابَلْتُ مُدِيرَ قِسْمِ اللُّغَاتِ صَبَاحاً. _____

٤- أنا وَصَدِيقِي نَتَدَرَّبُ عَلَىٰ لُعْبَةِ كُرَةِ السَّلَّة. _____

٥- شَارَكَ صَدِيقِي في سِبَاقِ السَّيَّارَاتِ السَّنَوِيّ. _____

٦- يُحَسِّنُ أخي العلاقاتِ بَيْنَ زُمَلائِه. _____

٧- أَسْتَمْتِعُ بِقِرَاءَةِ القِصَصِ التَّأْرِيخِيَّة. _____

٨- نَحْنُ نَتَكَلَّمُ اللُّغَةَ العَرَبِيَّةَ في كُلِّيَّةِ الآدَاب. _____

٩- أُحِبُّ أَنْ اشْتَرِكَ مَعَ الأَصْدِقَاء. _____

١٠- أَسْتَمِعُ إلىٰ أَخْبَارِ الرِّيَاضَةِ وأُشَاهِدُها على التِّلْفَازِ كُلَّ صَبَاح.

_____

XII-6. Select a derived verb from the table that best fits in the blanks. Pay attention to the correct conjugation of these verbs:

كَتَبَ	تَخَرَّجَ	تَدَرَّبَ trained	قابَلَ	يَذْهَبُ
دَرَّسَ	دَرَسَ	ساعَدَ	تَحَسَّنَ	إنْتَقَلَ

١- ــــــــــــــ كَريمٌ إلى الكُلِّيَّةِ بِسَيّارَتِهِ.

٢- الطّالِبُ ــــــــــــــ أُسْتاذَهُ في الجامِعَة.

٣- طَلَبَ الأُسْتاذُ مِن الطُّلّابِ أن ــــــــــــــ واجِبَ اللُّغَةِ العَرَبيَّةِ في الصَّفّ.

٤- ــــــــــــــ العِلاقاتُ بَيْنَ أفرادِ العائِلَة.

٥- أخي ــــــــــــــ اللُّغَةَ العَرَبيَّةَ في كُلِّيَةِ الأدَبِ العَرَبيِّ.

٦- ــــــــــــــ صَديقي إلى بَيْتٍ صَغيرٍ.

٧- ــــــــــــــ أُخْتي الكيمياءَ في المَدْرَسَةِ الثّانَويَّة.

٨- ــــــــــــــ أحْمَد مِن الكُلِّيَّةِ في فَصْلِ الرَّبيعِ الدِّراسِيّ.

٩- أنا وَأخي وَأُخْتي ــــــــــــــ والِدَتَنا دائِماً.

١٠- ــــــــــــــ عَلى عِلاجِ فَيروسِ الكَرونا في الكُلِّيَّةِ الطِّبّيَّة.

255

Notes

Section XIII: Arabic Vocabulary Puzzles 1-1 to 8-1

Puzzle #1-1

ACROSS
2-2 Monday
3-٣ My friends 'fp'
4-٤ Drills, Exercises

DOWN
1-١ The house
5-٥ News
6-٦ We read it.

Puzzle #2-1

١ شَ				٢ طَ	٣ يَ	٤ ف
				٥ أ		
٦ قَ						
٧ طُ						
٨ سَ						
٩ تَ						
١٠ دَ						

ACROSS

1-١ Street

6-٦ He read 'past'

7-٧ Students

8-٨ An hour, a watch

9-٩ She writes

10-١٠ Notebook

DOWN

2-٢ A bird

3-٣ They eat

4-٤ A team

5-٥ Professor

Puzzle #3-1

ACROSS

4-٤ I say
6-٦ Yes
7- ٧ Father
10 -١٠ Children
11-١١ Mothers
12-١٢ Annoyed 'm'

DOWN

1-١ Sad 'f'
2-٢ We learn
3-٣ The lesson
5-٥ Friends, companions
8-٨ Girls
9-٩ Happy 'f'

Puzzle #4-1 (‗ References two-word vocabulary)

ACROSS

1-١ Welcome
3-٣ Where are you 'm-f,p' ?
6-٦ My sister
7-٧ They play
8-٨ Exam
11-١١ We are honored by you 'f'
12-١٢ I eat chicken
13-١٣ An Arab
14-١٤ An Indian
15-١٥ I read a book
16- He
17-University student
18-Those are engineers

DOWN

2-٢ My friend
4-٤ With me
5-٥ He works
9-٩ House
10-١٠ He says

Puzzle #5-1

ACROSS
- 2-٢ Happy
- 3-٣ Went out
- 4-٤ Graduated
- 5-٥ College
- 6-٦ He writes
- 7-٧ This
- 8-٨ Pencil
- 9-٩ He runs away
- 10-١٠ I eat
- 11-١١ He heard
- 13-١٣ Worked
- 15-١٥ He
- 16-١٦ Who
- 20-٢٠ How much
- 21-٢١ Or
- 22-٢٢ Uncle (maternal)
- 23-٢٣ Thereupon

DOWN
- 1-١ My companion 'm'
- 12-١٢ Engineering
- 14-١٤ Library
- 17-١٧ Brothers and sisters
- 18-١٨ He wrote
- 19-١٩ He read 'past tense'

Puzzle #6-1

ACROSS		DOWN			
3-٣	He is happy	1-١	He runs	16-١٦ They watch	24-٢٤ We go
4-٤	We hear	2-٢	He sleeps	17-١٧ They work	25-٢٥ He studies
6-٦	He erased	5-٥	He takes	18-١٨ They	26-٢٦ She studies
7-٧	He goes out	8-٨	We	19-١٩ She	
9-٩	They advance 'm'	10-١٠	You 'f'	20-٢٠ They Listen	
11-١١	He delays	12-١٢	You eat 'f'	21-٢١ They study	
13-١٣	He laughed	14-١٤	They help	22-٢٢ They memorize	
		15-١٥	They travel	23-٢٣ They thank	

Puzzle # 7-1

ACROSS

5-٥ They
6-٦ Tree
8-٨ She
9-٩ Room
10-١٠ Window
13-١٣ Door
14-١٤ Building floors
16-١٦ College
19-١٩ Professor
22-٢٢ Schools
23-٢٣ Stars
25-٢٥ Sun
26-٢٦ Moon
27-٢٧ Sky

DOWN

1-١ Cars
2-٢ Streets
3-٣ Stores
4-٤ Buildings
7-٧ Offices
11-١١ Virus
12-١٢ Corona
15-١٥ Computer
17-١٧ City
18-١٨ States
20-٢٠ Center
21-٢١ Vaccine
24-٢٤ My Mother
25-٢٥ Father

Puzzle #8-1 (___ References two-word vocabulary)

ACROSS

2-٢ University
3-٣ classes
4-٤ Office
5-٥ An employee
6-٦ Laboratory
7-٧ Languages
9-٩ Soccer (2 words)
10-١٠ Field
11-١١ Games
13-١٣ Teacher 'f'
14-١٤ A language
17-١٧ A player
20-٢٠ Far away
21-٢١ Close by
22-٢٢ Names, Nouns

DOWN

1-١ Student
8-٨ Our factories
12-١٢ Workers, laborers
15-١٥ Coffee
16-١٦ Sciences
18-١٨ Sugar
19-١٩ Tea

Section XIV: Appendices

Appendix 1: Commonly Used Nouns

Noun codes:

Singular/plural (s/p), Feminine (f) , Masculine (m), Feminine regular plural (f-rp) masculine regular plural (m-rp), Feminine irregular plural (f-irrp)   Masculine irregular plural (m-irrp)

Table (1)   Commonly used nouns in Arabic and English:

English (singular/plural)	Arabic singular	Arabic plural
age/ages	عُمْر 'm'	أَعْمَار 'f – irrp'
airplane/s	طَائِرَة 'f'	طَائِرَات 'f – rp'
ant/s	نَمْلَة 'f'	نَمْل 'f – irrp'
bathroom/s	حَمَّام 'm'	حَمَّامَات 'f – rp'
bed/s	تَخْت ـ سَرِير 'm'	تُخُوْت / أَسِرَّة 'f – irrp'
bird/s	طَيْر 'm'	طُيُور 'f – irrp'
boat/s	قَارِب 'm'	قَوَارِب 'f – irrp'
book/s	كِتَاب 'm'	كُتُب 'f – irrp'
boy/s	وَلَد 'm'	أَوْلَاد 'm – irrp '

brother/s	أخ 'm'	إخْوَة 'm – irrp'
building/s	بِنَايَة 'f'	بِنَايَات 'f – rp'
bus/es	بَاص 'm'	بَاصَات 'f – rp'
car/s	سَيَّارَة 'f'	سَيَّارَات 'f – rp'
cat/s	قِطَّة 'f'	قِطَط 'f – irrp'
chair/s	كُرْسِيّ 'm'	كَرَاسِي 'f – irrp'
church/s	كَنِيسَة 'f'	كَنَائِس 'f – irrp'
city/cities	مَدِينَة 'f'	مُدُن 'f – irrp'
classmate/s, colleague/s	زَمِيل 'm'	زُمَلَاء 'm – irrp'
classmate/s, colleague/s	زَمِيلَة 'f'	زَمِيلَات 'f – rp'
clinic/s	عِيَادَة 'f'	عِيَادَات 'f – rp'
college/s	كُلِّيَّة 'f'	كُلِّيَّات 'f – rp'
country/countries	بَلَد 'm'	بِلَاد 'f – irrp'

daughter/s, girl/s	بِنْت/إبْنَة 'f'	بَنَات 'f – rp'
day/s	يَوْم 'm'	أَيَام 'f – irrp'
deer/s	غَزَالَة 'f'	غِزْلَان/ غَزَال 'f – irrp'
desert/s	صَحْرَاء 'f'	صَحَارِي 'f – irrp'
dog/s	كَلْب 'm'	كِلَاب 'f – irrp'
door/s	بَاب 'm'	أَبْوَاب 'f – irrp'
evening/s	مَسَاء 'm'	أُمْسِيَات 'f – rp'
face/s	وَجْه 'm'	وُجُوْه 'f – irrp'
family/families	أُسْرَة 'f'	أُسَر 'f – irrp'
family/families	عَائِلَة 'f'	عَائِلَات 'f – rp'
father/s	أب 'm'	آبَاء 'm – irrp'
foot/feet	قَدَم 'm'	أَقْدَام 'f – irrp'
form/s	شَكْل 'm'	أَشْكَال 'f – irrp'

English	Singular	Plural
fruit/s	فَاكِهَة 'f'	فَوَاكِه 'f – irrp'
garden/s	حَدِيْقَة 'f'	حَدَائِق 'f – irrp'
garment/s, apparel	رِدَاء 'm'	مَلَابِس 'f – irrp'
girl/s	بِنْت 'f'	بَنَات 'f – rp'
grandfather/s	جَدّ	أَجْدَاد 'm-irrp'
grandmother/s	جَدَّة 'f'	جَدَّات 'f – rp'
hill/s	تَل 'm'	تِلَال 'f – irrp'
home/s	دَار 'm'	دُوْر 'f – irrp'
hospital/s	مُسْتَشْفَى 'f'	مُسْتَشْفَيَات 'f – rp'
house/s	بَيْت 'm'	بُيُوت 'f – irrp'
key/s	مِفْتَاح 'm'	مَفَاتِيْح 'f – irrp'
kitchen/s	مَطْبَخ 'm'	مَطَابِخ 'f – irrp'
lady/ladies	سَيِّدة 'f'	سَيِّدات 'f – rp'

land/s	أَرْض 'f'	أَرَاضِي 'f - irrp'	
library/libraries	مَكْتَبَة 'f'	مَكْتَبَات 'f – rp'	
man/men	رَجُل 'm'	رِجَال 'm – irrp'	
market/s	سُوْق 'm'	أَسْوَاق 'f – irrp'	
Master/s (Mr.)	سَيِّد 'm'	سَادَة 'm-irrp'	
month/s	شَهْر 'm'	أَشْهُر/شُهُوْر 'f - irrp'	
moon/s	قَمَر 'm'	أَقْمَار 'f – irrp'	
mosque/s	مَسْجِد 'm'	مَسَاجِد 'f – irrp'	
mother/s	أُم 'f'	أُمَّهَات 'f - rp'	
mountain/s	جَبَل 'm'	جِبَال 'f – irrp'	
nation/s	أُمَّة 'f'	أُمَم 'f - irrp'	
night/s	لَيْل 'm'	لَيَالِي 'f - irrp'	
office/s	مَكْتَب 'm'	مَكَاتِب 'f - irrp'	

orange/s	بُرْتُقَالَة 'f'	بُرْتُقَال 'm- irrp'	
page/s	صَفْحَة 'f'	صَفَحَات 'f - rp'	
paper/s	وَرَقَة	أَوْرَاق 'f - irrp'	
pen/s	قَلَم حِبْر 'm'	أَقْلَام حِبْر 'f - irrp'	
pencil/s	قَلَم 'm'	أَقْلَام 'f - irrp'	
picture/s	صُوْرَة 'f'	صُوَر 'f - irrp'	
restaurant/s	مَطْعَم 'm'	مَطَاعِم 'f - irrp'	
river/s	نَهْر 'm'	أَنْهَار 'f - irrp'	
road/s	طَرِيْق 'm'	طُرُق 'f - irrp'	
room/s	غُرْفَة 'f'	غُرَف 'f - irrp'	
school /s	مَدْرَسَة 'f'	مَدَارِس 'f - irrp'	
sea/s	بَحْر 'm'	بِحَار 'f - irrp'	
ship/s	بَاخِرَة 'f'	بَوَاخِر 'f - irrp'	

sky/skies	سَمَاء 'f'	سَمَاوَات 'f - rp'
son/s	إبْن 'm'	أبْنَاء 'm - irrp'
star/s	نَجْمَة 'f'	نُجُوم 'f - irrp'
state/s	وِلَايَة 'f'	وِلَايَات 'f - rp'
street/s	شَارِع 'm'	شَوَارِع 'f - irrp'
sun/s	شَمْس 'f'	شُمُوس 'f - irrp'
table/s	طَاوِلَة 'f'	طَاوِلَات 'f - rp'
temple/s	مَعْبَد 'm'	مَعَابِد 'f - irrp'
train/s	قِطَار 'm'	قِطَارَات 'f - rp'
tree/s	شَجَرَة 'f'	أشْجَار 'f - irrp'
uncle/s	عَم 'm'	أعْمَام 'm - irrp'
university/universities	جَامِعَة 'f'	جَامِعَات 'f - rp'
water/s	مَاء 'm'	مِيَاه 'f - irrp'

weather/s	جَو 'm'	أَجْوَاء 'f - irrp'
week/s	أُسْبُوْع 'm'	أَسَابِيْع 'f - irrp'
window/s	شُبَّاك 'm'	شَبَابِيك 'f - irrp'
woman/women	إمْرَأة 'f'	نِسَاء ، نِسْوَة 'f - irrp'
year/s	سَنَة 'f'	سَنَوَات 'f – rp'

Notes

Appendix 2-A: Commonly Used Masculine Verbs
(3rd person singular هُوَ)

Table (2)

Masculine Past tense	الماضِي المُذَكَّر	Masculine present tense	المُضارِعُ المُذَكَّر
accepted	قَبِلَ	accepts	يَقْبَلُ
accommodated	وَفَّقَ بَيْنَ	accommodates	يُوَفِّقُ بَيْنَ
accomplished	حَقَّقَ	accomplishes	يُحَقِّقُ
added	أضَافَ	adds	يُضِيفُ
admitted	أقَرَّ	admits	يُقِرُّ
advised	أَرْشَدَ	advises	يُرْشِدُ
agreed with	إتَّفَقَ مَعَ	agrees with	يَتَّفِقُ مَعَ
alerted	حَذَّرَ	alerts	يُحَذِّرُ
allowed	سَمَحَ	allows	يَسْمَحُ
answered	أَجَابَ عَلـى	answers	يُجِيبُ عَلـى
appreciated his/her work	قَدَّرَ عَمَلَهُ/ عَمَلَها	appreciates his/her work	يُقَدِّرُ عَمَلَهُ/ عَمَلَها
ate	أكَلَ	eats	يَأكُلُ

began from	بَدَأَ مِن	begins from	يَبْدَأُ مِن
bought	إِشْتَرَىٰ	buys	يَشْتَرِي
came to	أَتَىٰ إِلَىٰ	comes to	يَأْتِي إِلَىٰ
collaborated with	تَعَاوَنَ مَعَ	collaborates with	يَتَعَاوَنُ مَعَ
confessed	إِعْتَرَفَ بِـ	confesses	يَعْتَرِفُ بِـ
connected with	إِتَّصَلَ بِـ	connects with	يَتَّصِلُ بِـ
decided on/upon	قَرَّرَ عَلَىٰ	decides on/upon	يُقَرِّرُ عَلَىٰ
demanded from	طَلَبَ مِن	demands from	يَطْلُبُ مِن
depended on/upon	إِعْتَمَدَ عَلَىٰ	depends on/upon	يَعْتَمِدُ عَلَىٰ
did	فَعَلَ	does	يَفْعَلُ
drank	شَرِبَ	drinks	يَشْرَبُ
drove the car	قَادَ السَّيَّارَة	drives the car	يَقُودُ السَّيَّارَة
educated	رَبَّىٰ	educates	يُرَبِّي

encouraged	شَجَّعَ	encourages	يُشَجِّعُ
ended	إنْتَهَى مِن	ends	يَنْتَهِي مِن
entered in	دَخَلَ فِي	enters in	يَدْخُلُ فِي
fed the hungry	أَطْعَمَ الجَائِعَ	feeds the hungry	يُطْعِمُ الجَائِعَ
forebode	نَهَى عَن	forbids	يَنْهَى عَن
found	وَجَدَ	finds	يَجِدُ
gave	أَعْطَى	gives	يُعْطِي
got	حَصَلَ عَلَى	gets	يَحْصُلُ عَلَى
got up	قَامَ/نَهَضَ	gets up	يَقُومُ/يَنْهَضُ
heard	سَمِعَ	hears	يَسْمَعُ
held	مَسَكَ	holds	يُمْسِكُ
left	تَرَكَ	leaves	يَتْرُكُ
listened to	إسْتَمَعَ إلى	listens to	يَسْتَمِعُ إلى

lived in	سَكَنَ فِي	lives in	يَسْكُنُ فِي
loved/liked	أَحَبَّ/ مَالَ إلى	likes	يُحِبُّ/ يَمِيْلُ إلى
memorized	حَفِظَ	memorizes	يَحْفِظُ
needed to	إحْتَاجَ إلى	needs to	يَحْتَاجُ إلى
played with	لَعِبَ مَعَ	plays with	يَلْعَبُ مَعَ
prevented	مَنَعَ	prevents	يَمْنَعُ
questioned	سَأَلَ	questions	يَسْأَلُ
ran to	رَكَضَ إلى	runs to	يَرْكُضُ إلى
ran away	هَرَبَ	runs away	يَهْرُبُ
read	قَرَأَ	reads	يَقْرَأُ
received a guest	إسْتَقْبَلَ ضَيْفاً	receives a guest	يَسْتَقْبِلُ ضَيْفاً
registered	سَجَّلَ	registered	يُسَجِّلُ
remembered	تَذَكَّرَ	remembers	يَتَذَكَّرُ
rescued	أَنْقَذَ	rescues	يُنْقِذُ
returned from	رَجَعَ مِن	returns from	يَرْجِعُ مِن

ruled	حَكَمَ	rules	يَحْكُمُ
said	قَالَ	says	يَقُولُ
sang	غَنَّى	sings	يُغَنِّي
sat	جَلَسَ	sits	يَجْلِسُ
slept	نَامَ	sleeps	يَنَامُ
smiled	إِبْتَسَمَ	smiles	يَبْتَسِمُ
sold	بَاعَ	sells	يَبِيعُ
spoke	تَكَلَّمَ	speaks	يَتَكَلَّمُ
started	بَدَأَ	starts	يَبْدَأُ
stayed	بَقَىٰ/ بَقِيَ	stays	يَبْقَىٰ
stopped	أَوْقَفَ	stops	يُوقِفُ
stored	خَزَنَ	stores	يَخْزِنُ
studied	دَرَسَ	studies	يَدْرُسُ
succeeded	نَجَحَ	succeeds	يَنْجَحُ

talked	تَحَدَّثَ	talks	يَتَحَدَّثُ
taught	دَرَّسَ	teaches	يُدَرِّسُ
thanked, him/her	شَكَرَهُ / شَكَرَها	thanks, him/her	يَشْكُرُهُ / يَشْكُرُهَا
thought	فَكَّرَ	thinks	يُفَكِّرُ
threw the ball	رَمَى الكُرَةَ	throws the ball	يَرْمِي الكُرَةَ
took	أَخَذَ	takes	يَأْخُذُ
trained on	تَدَرَّبَ عَلَى	trains on	يَتَدَرَّبُ عَلَى
traveled to	سَافَرَ إلى	travels to	يُسَافِرُ إلى
tried	حَاوَلَ	tries	يُحَاوِلُ
validated	صَادَقَ عَلَى	validates	يُصَادِقُ عَلَى
voted	صَوَّتَ	votes	يُصَوِّتُ
walked to	سَارَ إلى	walks to	يَسِيرُ إلى
walked to	مَشَى إلى	walks to	يَمْشِي إلى

wanted	أَرَادَ	wants	يُرِيدُ
warned	أَنْذَرَ / حَذَّرَ	warns	يُنْذِرُ / يُحَذِّرُ
washed	غَسَلَ	washes	يَغْسِلُ
watched	شَاهَدَ	watches	يُشَاهِدُ
welcomed	رَحَّبَ	welcomes	يُرَحِّبُ
went out from	خَرَجَ مِن	goes out from	يَخْرُجُ مِن
went to	ذَهَبَ إلى	goes to	يَذهَبُ إلى
whispered	هَمَسَ	whispers	يَهْمِسُ
woke up	إسْتَيْقَظَ	wakes up	يَسْتَيْقِظُ
won	رَبِحَ	wins	يَرْبَحُ
wondered about	تَعَجَّبَ - تَسَاءَلَ	wonders about	يَتَعَجَّبُ - يَتَسَاءَلُ
wore	لَبِسَ	wears	يَلْبِسُ
worked	عَمِلَ	works	يَعْمَلُ
worried	قَلِقَ	worries	يَقْلَقُ
wrote	كَتَبَ	writes	يَكْتُبُ

Appendix 2-B: Commonly Used Feminine Verbs
(3rd person singular هِيَ)

Table (3)

Feminine Past tense	الماضي المُؤنَّث	Feminine present tense	المُضارِعُ المُؤنَّث
accepted	قَبِلَت	accepts	تَقْبَلُ
accommodated	وَفَّقَت بَيْنَ	accommodates	تُوَفِّقُ بَيْنَ
accomplished	حَقَّقَت	accomplishes	تُحَقِّقُ
added	أَضَافَت	adds	تُضِيفُ
admitted	أَقَرَّت	admits	تُقِرُّ
advised	أَرْشَدَت	advises	تُرْشِدُ
agreed	إتَّفَقَت مَعَ	agrees	تَتَفِقُ مَعَ
alerted	حَذَّرَت	alerts	تُحَذِّرُ
allowed	سَمَحَت	allows	تَسْمَحُ
answered	أَجَابَت عَلَى	answers	تُجِيبُ عَلَى
appreciated his/her work	قَدَّرَت عَمَلَهُ/ عَمَلَها	appreciates his/her work	تُقَدِّرُ عَمَلَهُ/ عَمَلَها
ate	أَكَلَت	eats	تَأْكُلُ

began from	بَدَأَت مِن	begins from	تَبْدَأُ مِن
bought	إشْتَرت	buys	تَشْتَري
came to	أَتَت إلىٰ	comes to	تَأتِي إلىٰ
collaborated with	تَعَاوَنَت مَعَ	collaborates with	تَتَعَاوَنُ مَعَ
confessed	إعْتَرَفَت بِـ	confesses	تَعْتَرِفُ بِـ
connected with	إتَّصَلَت بِـ	connects with	تَتَّصِلُ بِـ
decided on/upon	قَرَّرَت عَلىٰ	decides on/upon	تُقَرِّرُ عَلىٰ
demanded from	طَلَبَت مِن	demands from	تَطْلُبُ مِن
depended on/upon	إعْتَمَدَت عَلىٰ	depends on/upon	تَعْتَمِدُ عَلىٰ
did	فَعَلَت	does	تَفْعَلُ
drank	شَرِبَت	drinks	تَشْرَبُ
drove	قَادَت	drives	تَقُودُ
educated/raised	رَبَّت	educates/raises	تُرَبِّي

encouraged	شَجَّعَت	encourages	تُشَجِّعُ
ended/finished	إنْتَهَت مِن	ends/finishes	تَنْتَهِي مِن
entered in	دَخَلَت فِي	enters in	تَدْخُلُ فِي
fed the needy	أطْعَمَت الجَائِعَ	feeds the needy	تُطْعِمُ الجَائِعَ
found	وَجَدَت	finds	تَجِدُ
forbode	نَهَت عَن	forbids	تَنْهى عَن
gave	أَعْطَت	gives	تُعْطِي
got	حَصَلَت عَلى	gets	تَحْصُلُ عَلى
got up	قَامَت/نَهَضَت	gets up	تَقُومُ/تَنْهَضُ
heard	سَمِعَت	hears	تَسْمَعُ
held	مَسَكَت	holds	تُمْسِكُ
left	تَرَكَت	leaves	تَتْرُكُ
liked/loved	أَحَبَّت، مالَت إلى	likes	تُحِبُّ، تَمِيلُ إلى
listened	إسْتَمَعَت	listens	تَسْتَمِعُ

lived in	سَكَنَت فِي	lives in	تَسْكُنُ فِي
memorized	حَفِظَت	memorizes	تَحْفِظُ
needed to	إحْتَاجَت إلى	needs to	تَحْتَاجُ إلى
played with	لَعِبَت مَعَ	plays with	تَلْعَبُ مَعَ
prevented	مَنَعَت	prevents	تَمْنَعُ
questioned	سَألَت	questions	تَسْألُ
ran to	رَكَضَت إلى	runs to	تَرْكُضُ إلى
ran away	هَرَبَت	runs away	تَهْرُبُ
read	قَرَأَت	reads	تَقْرَأُ
received a guest	إسْتَقْبَلَت ضَيْفاً	receives a guest	تَسْتَقْبِلُ ضَيْفاً
registered	سَجَّلَت	registers	تُسَجِّلُ
ruled	حَكَمَت	rules	تَحْكُمُ
said	قَالَت	says	تَقُولُ
sang	غَنَّت	sings	تُغَنِّي
sat	جَلَسَت	sits	تَجْلِسُ

slept	نَامَت	sleeps	تَنَامُ
smiled	إبْتَسَمَت	smiles	تَبْتَسِمُ
sold	بَاعَت	sells	تَبِيعُ
spoke	تَكَلَّمَت	speaks	تَتَكَلَّمُ
started	بَدَأَت	starts	تَبْدَأُ
stayed	بَقَت/ بَقِيَت	stays	تَبْقَى
stopped	أَوْقَفَت	stops	تُوقِفُ
stored	خَزَنَت	stores	تَخْزِنُ
studied	دَرَسَت	studies	تَدْرُسُ
succeeded	نَجَحَت	succeeds	تَنْجَحُ
talked	تَكَلَّمَت ـ تَحَدَّثَت	talks	تَتَكَلَّمُ ـ تَتَحَدَّثُ
taught	دَرَّسَت	teaches	تُدَرِّسُ
thanked, him/her	شَكَرَتْهُ/ شَكَرَتْهَا	thanks, him/her	تَشْكُرُهُ / تَشْكُرُهَا
thought	فَكَّرَت	thinks	تُفَكِّرُ

threw the ball	رَمَت الكُرَةَ	throws the ball	تَرمِي الكُرَةَ
took	أَخَذَت	takes	تَأْخُذُ
trained on	تَدَرَّبَت عَلَى	trains on	تَتَدَرَّبُ عَلَى
traveled to	سَافَرَت إِلَى	travels to	تُسَافِرُ إِلَى
tried	حَاوَلَت	tries	تُحَاوِلُ
validated	صَادَقَت عَلَى	validates	تُصَادِقُ عَلَى
voted	صَوَّتَت	votes	تُصَوِّتُ
walked to	سَارَت إِلَى	walks to	تَسِيرُ إِلَى
walked to	مَشَت إِلَى	walks to	تَمْشِي إِلَى
wanted	أَرَادَت	wants	تُرِيدُ
washed	غَسَلَت	washes	تَغْسِلُ
watched	شَاهَدَت	watches	تُشَاهِدُ
welcomed	رَحَّبَت	welcomes	تُرَحِّبُ
went out from	خَرَجَت مِن	goes out from	تَخْرُجُ مِن

went to	ذَهَبَت إلى	goes to	تَذهَبُ إلى
whispered	هَمَسَت	whispers	تَهمِسُ
woke up	إسْتَيْقَظَت	wakes up	تَسْتَيْقِظُ
won	رَبِحَت	wins	تَربَحُ
wondered about	تَعَجَّبَت - تَسَاءَلت	wonders about	تَتَعَجَّبُ - تَتَسَاءَلُ
wore	لَبِسَت	wears	تَلبِسُ
worked	عَمِلَت	works	تَعمَلُ
worried	قَلِقَت	worries	تَقلَقُ
wrote	كَتَبَت	writes	تَكْتُبُ

Notes:

Appendix 3: Standard Conjugation of the Past Verb

1st, 2nd, 3rd person pronouns

Example: (went) ذَهَبَ

Table (3-A) Conjugation of the past verb:

Verb	1st person pronoun	2nd person pronoun	3rd person pronoun
I went	أنا ذَهَبْتُ		
we went	نَحْنُ ذَهَبْنَا		
you went 'ms'		أنْتَ ذَهَبْتَ	
you went 'fs'		أنْتِ ذَهَبْتِ	
you went 'm-f, dual'		أنْتُمَا ذَهَبْتُمَا	
you went 'm-f, p'		أنْتُم ذَهَبْتُم	
you went 'fp'		أنْتُنَّ ذَهَبْتُنَّ	
he went 'm'			هُوَ ذَهَبَ
she went 'f'			هِيَ ذَهَبَت
they went 'm-f, dual'			هُمَا ذَهَبَا
they went 'm-f, p'			هُم ذَهَبُوا
they went 'fp'			هُنَّ ذَهَبْنَ

Table (3-B) Past verb conjugation for proper nouns:

proper nouns	1st person proper noun	2nd person proper noun	3rd person proper noun
I am, Semer went	"أنا سَمَر" ذَهَبْتُ		
I am, Kareem went	"أنا كَرِيْم" ذَهَبْتُ		
we, Semer and Kareem went 'm-f,dual'	"نَحْنُ سَمَر و كَرِيْم" ذَهَبْنَا		
we Semer, and Kareem, and Maryam went 'm-f,p'	"نَحْنُ سَمَر و كَرِيْم ومَرْيَم" ذَهَبْنَا		
we Semer, and Mariam, and Reem went 'fp'	"نَحْنُ سَمَر ومَرْيَم وريم" ذَهَبْنَا		
Kareem, you went, 'ms'		"كَرِيْم أنْتَ" ذَهَبْتَ	
Semer, you went 'fs'		"سَمَر أنْتِ" ذَهَبْتِ	
Semer and Kareem, you went 'm-f,dual'		"سَمَر وَ كَرِيْم أنْتُمَا" ذَهَبْتُمَا	
Semer, and Kareem, and, Mariam you went 'm-f,p'		"سَمَر وَ كَرِيْم ومَرْيَم أنتم" ذَهَبْتُم	
Semer, and Maryam, and Reem, you went 'fp'		"سَمَر ومَرْيَم و ريم أنْتُنَّ" ذَهَبْتُنَّ	

Kareem went 'm'			"كَرِيْم" ذَهَب
Mariam went 'f'			"مَرَيَم" ذَهَبَت
Semer and Kareem went 'm-f, dual'			"سَمَر و كَرِيْم" ذَهَبا
Semer, and Kareem, and Reem went 'm-f,p'			"سَمَر وكَرِيْم و رِيم" ذَهَبُوا
Semer, and Maryam, and Reem went 'fp'			"سَمَر ومَرَيَم و رِيم" ذَهَبْنَ

Notes:

Appendix 4: Standard Conjugation of the Present Verb

Present verb conjugation for 1st, 2nd, and 3rd person subject

Example: goes يَذْهَبُ

Table (4-A) Conjugation of the present verb:

Verb	1st person pronoun (speaking)	2nd person pronoun (spoken to)	3rd person pronoun (spoken about)
I go/I am going	أَذْهَبُ "أنا"		
we go/we are going	نَـذْهَبُ "نَحْنُ"		
you go/are going 'ms'		تَـذْهَبُ "أَنْتَ"	
you go/are going 'fs'		تَـذْهَبِينَ "أَنْتِ"	
you go/are going 'm-f, dual'		تَذْهَبَان "أَنْتُمَا"	
you go/are going 'mp'		تَـذْهَبُونَ "أَنْتُم"	
you go/are going 'fp'		تَـذْهَبْنَ "أَنْتُنَّ"	
he goes/is going 'm'			يَـذْهَبُ "هُوَ"
she goes/is going 'f'			تَـذْهَبُ "هِيَ"
they go/are going 'm-f, dual'			يَـذْهَبُ "هُمَا"
they go/are going 'mp'			يَـذْهَبُ "هُم"
they go/are going 'fp'			يَـذْهَبْنَ "هُنَّ"

Table (4-B) Standard conjugation of the present verb:

proper nouns	1st person proper noun (speaking)	2nd person proper noun (spoken to)	3rd person proper noun (subject)
I, Kareem am going I, Semer am going	أذْهَبُ "أنا كَرِيْم" أذْهَبُ "أنا سَمَر"		
We, Kareem and Semer are going	نَذْهَبُ "نَحْنُ كَرِيْم وسَمَر"		
We, Kareem and Semer and Mariam, are going	نَذْهَبُ "نَحْنُ كَرِيْم وسَمَر ومَرِيَم"		
Kareem, you, are going 'ms'		تَذْهَبُ "أنتَ كَرِيْم"	
Mariam, you, are going 'fs'		تَذْهَبِيْن "أنتِ مَرِيَم"	
Kareem and Mariam, you, are going 'f-m,dual'		تَذْهَبَان "أنتُمَا كَرِيْم ومَرِيَم"	
Kareem and Mariam and Semer, you, are going 'f-m, p'		تَذْهَبُون "أنتُم كَرِيْم وَ مَرِيَم وسَمَر"	
Mariam and Semer and Reem, you, are going 'fp'		تَذْهَبْنَ "أنتُنَّ مَرِيَم وسَمَر ورِيْم"	
Kareem goes 'm'			يَذْهَبُ كَرِيْم
Mariam goes 'f'			تَذْهَبُ مَرِيَم
Kareem and Mariam are going 'm-f, dual'			يَذْهَبُ كَرِيْم ومَرِيَم
Kareem and Semer and Mariam are going 'mp'			يَذْهَبُ كَرِيْم وسَمَر ومَرِيَم
Mariam and Semer and Reem are going 'fp'			تَذْهَبُ مَرِيَم وسَمَر ورِيْم

Table (4-C) Standard conjugation of the verb preceded by pronoun subject. The verb "worked/works" عَمِلَ / يَعْمَلُ:

Verb	Past	present
I worked/work 'm-f,s'	أنا عَمِلْتُ	أنا أَعْمَلُ
we worked/work 'm-f,p'	نَحْنُ عَمِلْنَا	نَحْنُ نَعْمَلُ
you worked/work 'ms'	أنتَ عَمِلْتَ	أنتَ تَعْمَلُ
you worked/work 'fs'	أنتِ عَمِلْتِ	أنتِ تَعْمَلِين
you worked/work 'm-f,dual'	أنْتُمَا عَمِلْتُمَا	أنْتُمَا تَعْمَلان
you worked/work 'm-f,p'	أنْتُم عَمِلْتُم	أنْتُم تَعْمَلُون
you worked/work 'fp'	أنْتُنَّ عَمِلْتُنَّ	أنْتُنَّ تَعْمَلْنَ
he worked/work 'ms'	هُوَ عَمِلَ	هُوَ يَعْمَلُ
she worked/works 'fs'	هِيَ عَمِلَت	هِيَ تَعْمَلُ
they worked 'm'/work 'f, dual/work	هُمَا عَمِلَا/هُمَا عَمِلَتَا	هُمَا يَعْمَلان/ هُمَا تَعْمَلان
they worked/work 'm-f,p'	هُم عَمِلُوا	هُم يَعْمَلُون
they worked/work 'fp'	هُنَّ عَمِلْنَ	هُنَّ يَعْمَلْنَ

Notes:

Appendix 5: Commonly Used Adjectives

(MF*) masculine-feminine singular /plural, (FS/P**) feminine singular/plural, (MS/P***) masculine singular/plural

MF*	FS/P **	MS/P***
active/activists	نَشِيطَة/نَشِيطَات - نَاشِطَات	نَشِيط/نَاشِطُون
advisor/s	مُرْشِدَة/مُرْشِدَات	مُرْشِد/ مُرْشِدُون
beautiful	جَمِيلَة/جَمِيلَات	جَمِيْل/ جَمِيلُون
big	كَبِيْرَة/كَبِيْرَات	كَبِيْر/ كِبَار
busy	مَشْغُولَة/ مَشْغُولَات	مَشْغُول/ مَشْغُولُون
Democrat/s	دِيمُقْراطِيَّة/دِيمُوقْراطِيَّات	دِيمُقْراطِيّ/دِيمُوقْراطِيُّون
doctor/s	دُكْتُورَة/ دُكْتُورَات	دُكْتُور/ دَكاتِرَة
Egyptian/s	مِصْرِيَّة/مِصْرِيَّات	مِصْرِيّ/مِصْرِيُّون
fat	سَمِينَة/سَمِينَات	سَمِين/سِمَان
foreign student/s	طَالِبَة أَجْنَبِيَّة / طَالِبَات أَجْنَبِيَّات	طَالِب أَجْنَبِيّ/طُلَّاب أَجَانِب
happy	سَعِيْدَة/سَعِيْدَات	سَعِيْد/سُعَدَاء
hard worker/s	مُجْتَهِدَة/مُجْتَهِدَات	مُجْتَهِد/ مُجْتَهِدُون
healthy	صِحِّيَّة/صِحِّيَّات	صِحِّيّ/أَصِحَّاء

		English
عَالِي/عَالُون	عَالِيَة/عَالِيَات	high
مُسْتَقِل/ مُسْتَقِلُون	مُسْتَقِلَّة/مُسْتَقِلَّات	Independent/s
ذَكِيّ/أَذْكِيَاء	ذَكِيَّة/ذَكِيَّات	intelligent
عَالَمِيّ/ عَالَمِيُّون ـ دَوْلِيّ/ دَوْلِيُّون	عَالَمِيَّة/ عَالَمِيَّات ـ دَوْلِيَّة/ دَوْلِيَّات	International/Global
أُسْتَاذٌ عَالَمِيّ/أَسَاتِذَة عَالَمِيُّون	أُسْتَاذَة عَالَمِيَّة/ أُسْتَاذَات عَالَمِيَّات	International professor/s
عِراقِيّ/عِراقِيُّون	عِراقِيَّة/عِراقِيَّات	Iraqi/s
كَسْلَان/كُسَالَى	كَسْلَانَة/كَسْلَانَات	lazy
لُبْنَانِيّ/لُبْنَانِيُّون	لُبْنَانِيَّة/لُبْنَانِيَّات	Lebanese
طَوِيل/طِوال	طَوِيلَة/ طَوِيلَات	long /tall
تَاجِر/تُجَّار	تَاجِرَة/تاجِرَات	merchant/s
مَغْرِبِيّ/ مَغْرِبِيُّون، مَغَارِبَة	مغْرِبِيَّة/ مَغْرِبِيَّات	Moroccan/s
جَدِيد/جُدُد	جَدِيدَة/جَدِيدَات	new
طَيِّب/ طَيِّبُون	طَيِّبَة/طَيِّبَات	nice

overweight	ضَخِمَة/ضَخِمَات	ضَخْم/ضِخَام
poor	فَقِيْرَة/فَقِيْرَات	فَقِيْر/فُقَرَاء
reader/s	قَارِئَة/قَارِئَات	قَارِئ/قُرَّاء
Republican/s	جُمْهُورِيَّة/جُمْهُورِيَّات	جُمْهُورِيّ/جُمْهُورِيُّون
rich	غَنِيَّة/غَنِيَّات	غَنِيّ/أَغْنِيَاء
Saudi/s	سُعُودِيَّة/سُعُودِيَّات	سُعُودِيّ/سُعُودِيُّون
short	قَصِيْرَة/قَصِيْرَات	قَصِيْر/قِصَار
sick	مَرِيْضَة/مَرِيْضَات	مَرِيْض/مَرْضَى
slim	نَحِيْفَة/نَحِيْفَات	نَحِيْف/نِحَاف
small	صَغِيْرَة/صَغِيْرَات	صَغِيْر/صِغَار
stranger/s	غَرِيْبَة/غَرِيْبَات	غَرِيْب/غُرَبَاء
strong	قَوِيَّة/قَوِيَّات	قَوِيّ/أَقْوِيَاء
student/s	طَالِبَة/طَالِبَات	طَالِب/طُلَّاب
Syrian/s	سُورِيَّة/سُورِيَّات	سُورِيّ/سُورِيُّون

teacher/s	مُدَرِّسَة/مُدَرِّسَات	مُدَرِّس/مُدَرِّسُون
translator/s	مُتَرْجِمَة/مُتَرْجِمَات	مُتَرْجِم/مُتَرْجِمُون
weak	ضَعِيْفَة/ضَعِيْفَات	ضَعِيْف/ضُعَفَاء
wise	حَكِيْمَة، عَاقِلَة/حَكِيْمَات، عَاقِلَات	حَكِيْم، عَاقِل/ حُكَمَاء، عُقَلَاء
wrestler/s	مُصَارِعَة/مُصَارِعَات	مُصَارِع/مُصَارِعُون
writer/s	كَاتِبَة/كَاتِبَات	كَاتِب/كُتَّاب

Notes:

Appendix 6: Commonly used Opposite Adjectives

Column 1	Column 2	Column 3	Column 4
black	أَسْوَد	white	أَبْيَض
civil	مُهَذَّب	uncivil – ill mannered	غَيْر مُهَذَّب ـ غَيْر مُؤَدَّب
dark	ظَلَام	light	ضِيَاء
empty	فَارِغ	full	مَلآن
friend	صَدِيْق	enemy	عَدُوّ
happy	سَعِيْد	sad	حَزِيْن
hard	صَعْب	easy	سَهْل
healthy	صِحّيّ	sick	مَرِيْض
heavy	ثَقِيْل	light	خَفِيْف
hot	حَار	cold	بَارِد
he feels **hot**	حَرَّان	he feels **cold**	بَرْدَان
humid	رَطِب	dry	جَاف

Lazy, lethargic	خَامِل، كَسْلَان	vigorous, energetic	نَشِيط، فَعَّال
near	قَرِيْب	far	بَعِيْد
new	جَدِيْد	old	قَدِيْم
no, nay	لا، كَلَّا	yes, agreed	نَعَم، مُوَافِق
opened	مَفْتُوح	closed	مَغْلُوق، مُغْلَق
right, he is right	هو صَحِيْح	he is wrong	هُوَ غَلْطَان / مُخْطِئ
short	قَصِيْر	long	طَوِيْل
simple	بَسِيْط	complicated	مُعَقَّد
slow	بَطِئ	fast	سَرِيْع
small	صَغِيْر	big	كَبِيْر
strong	قَوِيّ	weak	ضَعِيْف
sunny	مُشْمِس	cloudy	غَائِم
tight-narrow	ضَيِّق	broad-wide	وَاسِع ـ عَرِيْض
tired	تَعْبَان	active/energetic	نَشِيْط

ugly	قَبِيْح	beautiful	جَمِيْل
under - down	تَحْت	above - up	فَوْق
winner	رَابِح	loser	خَاسِر

Notes:

Appendix 7: Commonly Used Adjective Phrases

Adjective-noun phrase	Singular adjective phrase	Plural adjective phrase
the active girl/s, activist/s 'f'	البِنْتُ النَّشِيطَةُ/النَّاشِطَةُ	البَنَاتُ النَّشِيطَاتُ/ النَّاشِطَاتُ
the American scientist/s 'm'	العَالِمُ الأَمرِيْكِيُّ	العُلَمَاءُ الأَمْرِيْكِيُّون
the American university/ universities 'f'	الجَامِعَةُ الأَمْرِيْكِيَّةُ	الجَامِعَاتُ الأَمْرِيْكِيَّةُ
the Arab girl/s 'f'	البِنْتُ العَرَبِيَّةُ	البَنَاتُ العَرَبِيَّاتُ
the Arabic country/countries	البَلَدُ العَرَبِيُّ 'm'	البِلَادُ العَرَبِيَّةُ 'fp'
the Arabic library/libraries 'f'	المَكْتَبَةُ العَرَبِيَّةُ	المَكْتَبَاتُ العَرَبِيَّةُ
the big apartment/s 'f'	الشَّقَّةُ الكَبِيرَةُ	الشُّقَقُ الكَبِيرَةُ
the crowded street/s 'm'	الشَّارِعُ المُزدَحِمُ 'm'	الشَّوارِعُ المُزدَحِمَةُ 'fp'
the electric car/s 'f'	السَّيَّارَةُ الكَهْرَبَائِيَّةُ	السَّيَّارَاتُ الكَهْرَبَائِيَّةُ
the foreign language/s 'f'	اللُّغَةُ الأَجْنَبِيَّةُ	اللُّغَاتُ الأَجْنَبِيَّةُ
the green door/s 'm'	البَابُ الأَخْضَرُ 'm'	الأَبْوابُ الخَضْرَاءُ 'fp'
the green tree/s 'f'	الشَّجَرَةُ الخَضْرَاءُ	الشَّجَرُ الأَخْضَرُ
the hard-working girl/s 'f'	البِنْتُ المُجْتَهِدَةُ	البَنَاتُ المُجْتَهِدَاتُ
the hard-working student/s 'm'	الطَّالِبُ المُجْتَهِدُ	الطُّلَّابُ المُجْتَهِدُونَ

the hard-working student/s 'f'	الطَّالِبَةُ المُجْتَهِدَةُ		الطَّالِبَاتُ المُجْتَهِدَاتُ
the high-rise building /s 'f'	البِنَايَةُ العَالِيَةُ		البِنَايَاتُ العَالِيَةُ
the intelligent boy/s 'm'	الوَلَدُ الذَّكِيُّ		الأَوْلَادُ الأَذْكِيَاءُ
the intelligent student /s 'm'	الطَّالِبُ الذَّكِيُّ		الطُّلَّابُ الأَذْكِيَاءُ
the intelligent student /s 'f'	الطَّالِبَةُ الذَّكِيَّةُ		الطَّالِبَاتُ الذَّكِيَّاتُ
the Japanese computer /s	الحَاسُوبُ اليَابَانِيُّ	'ms'	الحَوَاسِيبُ اليَابَانِيَّةُ 'fp'
the large room/s 'f'	الغُرْفَةُ الوَاسِعَةُ		الغُرَفُ الوَاسِعَةُ
the kind father/s 'm'	الوَالِدُ/الأَبُ الطَّيِّبُ		الآبَاءُ الطَّيِّبُون
the kind mother/s 'f'	الوَالِدَةُ/الأُمُّ الطَّيِّبَةُ		الوَالِدَاتُ/الأُمَّهَاتُ الطَّيِّبَاتُ
the modern house/houses 'm'	البَيْتُ الحَدِيثُ 'ms'		البُيُوتُ الحَدِيثَةُ 'fp'
my modern house/our modern houses 'm'	بَيْتِي الحَدِيثُ 'ms'		بُيُوتُنَا الحَدِيثَةُ 'fp'
the narrow street/s 'm'	الشَّارِعُ الضَّيِّقُ 'ms'		الشَّوَارِعُ الضَّيِّقَةُ 'fp'
his/their new books 'm'	كِتَابُهُ الجَدِيدُ 'ms'		كُتُبُهُم الجَدِيدَةُ 'fp'
the new professor/s	الأُسْتَاذُ الجَدِيدُ 'ms'		الأَسَاتِذَةُ الجُدُدُ 'mp'
the new professor/s 'f'	الأُسْتَاذَةُ الجَدِيدَةُ		الأُسْتَاذَاتُ الجَدِيدَاتُ
my old book/s 'm'	كِتَابِي القَدِيمُ 'ms'		كُتُبِي القَدِيمَةُ 'fp'
her old house/s 'm'	بَيْتُهَا القَدِيمُ 'ms'		بُيُوتُهَا القَدِيمَةُ 'fp'

the old student/s 'm'	الطَّالِبُ القَدِيمُ	الطُّلَّابُ القُدَامَى
the red car/cars 'f'	السَّيَّارَةُ الحَمْراءُ	السَّيَّارَاتُ الحَمْراءُ
the Saudi boy/s 'm'	الوَلَدُ السُّعُودِيُّ	الأَوْلادُ السُّعُودِيُّون
the Saudi girl/s 'f'	البِنْتُ السُّعُودِيَّةُ	البَنَاتُ السُّعُودِيَّاتُ
the schoolbook/s 'm'	الكِتابُ المَدْرَسِيُّ 'ms'	الكُتُبُ المَدْرَسِيَّةُ 'fp'
the small apartment/s 'f'	الشُّقَّةُ الصَّغِيرَةُ	الشُّقَقُ الصَّغِيرَةُ
the spacious house/s 'm'	البَيْتُ الوَاسِعُ 'm'	البُيُوتُ الوَاسِعَةُ 'fp'
the useful sentence/s 'f'	الجُمْلَةُ المُفِيدَةُ	الجُمَلُ المُفِيدَةُ
the website/s 'f'	الشَّبَكَةُ العَنْكَبُوتِيَّةُ	الشَّبَكَاتُ العَنْكَبُوتِيَّةُ
the white wall/s 'm'	الحَائِطُ الأَبْيَضُ 'ms'	الحِيطَانُ البَيْضَاءُ 'fp'

Notes:

Appendix 8: Commonly Used Idafa Phrases

airplane of the Middle East/ The Middle East Airplane	طَائِرَةُ ٱلشَّرْقِ ٱلأَوْسَط
bill of electricity/the electricity bill	قَائِمَةُ ٱلكَهْرَبَاء
books of the language's lab/the languages lab books	كُتُبُ مُخْتَبَرِ ٱللُّغَات
book of physics/the physics book	كِتَابُ ٱلفِيزْيَاء
car of my cousin/my cousin's car	سَيَّارَةُ ٱبْنِ عَمِّي
car of my brother/my brother's car	سَيَّارَةُ أَخِي
center of the computer/ computer center	مَرْكَزُ ٱلحَاسُوب
City of Rockville/Rockville City	مَدِينَةُ رُوكْفِيل
class of Arabic Language/the Arabic Language class	صَفُّ اللُّغَةِ العَرَبِيَّة
the disease of the heart/the heart disease	مَرَضُ ٱلقَلْب
the employee of the post office/ the post office employee	مُوَظَّفُ ٱلبَرِيد
family of our mother/our mother's family	أُسْرَةُ وَالِدَتِنَا
family of my father/my father's family	عَائِلَةُ وَالِدِي
factory of the cars/the car factory	مَصْنَعُ ٱلسَّيَّارَات
food of the restaurant/the restaurant's food	طَعَامُ ٱلمَطْعَم
grades of the students/the students' grades	دَرَجَاتُ الطُّلَّاب

house of his maternal uncle/his maternal uncle's house	بَيْتُ خَالِه
hospital of Cancer/the Cancer hospital	مُسْتَشْفَى ٱلسَّرَطَان
house of my father/ my father's house	بَيْتُ وَالِدِي
Infection of Corona-19/ Corona-19 Infection	إلْتِهَابُ ٱلكَرُونَا-١٩
jungles of the Amazon/the Amazon jungles	غَابَاتُ ٱلأَمَازُون
the lesson of Nursing/the Nursing lesson	دَرْسُ ٱلتَّمْرِيض
library of the college/ the college library	مَكْتَبَةُ ٱلكُلِّيَّة
library of the university/the university library	مَكْتَبَةُ ٱلجَامِعَة
map of the world/the world's map	خَارِطَةُ ٱلعَالَم
the market of the fish/the fish market	سُوقُ ٱلسَّمَك
media of social communication/the social media communication	شَبَكَةُ ٱلتَّوَاصُلِ ٱلإِجْتِمَاعِي
number of my house/my house number	رَقْمُ بَيْتِي
number of my telephone/my telephone number	رَقْمُ تَلِيفُونِي
office of the university president/the university president's office	مَكْتَبُ رَئِيسِ ٱلجَامِعَة
the president of the college/the college president	رَئِيسُ ٱلكُلِّيَّة
principal of the school/the school's principal	مُدِيرُ ٱلمَدْرَسَة
professors of the university/the university professors	أَسَاتِذَةُ ٱلجَامِعَة

restaurant of the falafel/the falafel restaurant	مَطْعَمُ ٱلْفَلَافِل
room of my sister/my sister's room	غُرفَةُ أُخْتِي
State of Texas/Texas State	وِلايَةُ تَكْسَاس
station of the railway/the railway station	مَحطَّةُ ٱلْقِطَار
street of my house/my house street	شَارِعُ بَيْتِي
student of the college/the college student	طَالِبُ ٱلْكُلِّيَّة
test of the admission/the admission's test	إمْتِحَانُ ٱلْقُبُول
treatment of the Corona-19/ the Corona-19 treatment	عِلاجُ ٱلْكَرُونَا-١٩
the vaccine of the Corona-19/ Corona-19 vaccine	لُقَاحُ ٱلْكَرُونَا-١٩

Notes:

Appendix 9: Commonly Used Colors

English	Masculine	Feminine
black	أَسْوَد	سَوْداء
blue	أَزْرَق	زَرْقاء
brown	بُنِّيّ	بُنِّيَة
dark blue	أَزْرَق غَامِق	زَرْقاء غَامِقة
dark green	أَخْضَر غَامِق	خَضْراء غَامِقة
green	أَخْضَر	خَضْراء
grey	رَمادِيّ	رَمادِيَّة
hot pink	وَرْدِيّ غَامِق	وَرْدِيَّة غَامِقة
light blue	أَزْرَق فَاتِح	زَرْقاء فَاتِحة
orange	بُرْتْقَالِيّ	بُرْتْقَالِيَّة
pink	وَرْدِيّ	وَرْدِيَّة
purple	بَنَفْسَجِيّ	بَنَفْسَجِيَّة
red	أَحْمَر	حَمْراء
white	أَبْيَض	بَيْضاء
yellow	أَصْفَر	صَفْراء

Notes:

Appendix 10: Commonly Used Prepositions and Adverbs

above	فَوقَ
about/away from	عَن
behind	وَرَاء
by	بِـ
for or to	لِـ
from	مِن
in	فِي
in between	بَيْنَ
in front	أَمَامَ
on/above	عَلـىٰ
on top of	فَوقَ
to	إلـىٰ
under	تَحْتَ
until	حَتّـىٰ
with	مَعَ

Appendix 11: Most Commonly Attached Pronoun Suffixes to Prepositions and Adverbs

pronouns	English meaning	Prepositions - Adverbs	English meaning	attached suffix	English meaning
ـنَا	us	بَيْنَ	in between	بَيْنَنَا	between us
ـنَا	us	وَرَاءَ	behind	وَرَاءَنَا	behind us
ـكِ / ـكَ	you 'm-f,s'	بِجَانِبْ	with, by, beside, next to	بكِ، بكَ بِجَانِبِكَ بِجَانِبِكِ	with you, by you, beside you, next to you
ـكُم	you (plural)	عَلَىٰ	on	عَلَيْكُم	upon you 'm-f,p'
ـكُم	you (plural)	إِلَىٰ	to	إِلَيْكُم	to you 'm-f,p'
ـكُم	you (plural)	أَمَامَ	in front	أَمَامَكُم	in front of you
ـهُ / ـهَا	him/her	فِي	in	فِيهَا ، فِيهِ	in it 'f-m'
ـهُ / ـهَا	him/her	مِن	from	مِنْهُ ، مِنْهَا	from /him, her
ـهُ / ـهَا	him/her	مَعَ	with	مَعَهُ ، مَعَهَا	with him with her
ـهُم	them	فَوْقَ	above	فَوْقَهُم	above them
ـهُم	them	تَحْتَ	under	تَحْتَهُم	under them

Notes:

Appendix 12: Commonly Used Preposition and Adverb Phrases

away from people	بَعِيْداً عَنِ ٱلنَّاس
beside him/her	بِجَانِيهِ / بِجَانِيهَا
beside them 'm/f'	بِجَانِيهِم/بِجَانِيهِنَّ
from behind him/her	مِن وَرَاءِهِ/ مِن وَرَائِهَا
from the store	مِنَ ٱلمَخْزَن
in between the lines	بَيْنَ ٱلسُّطُور
in front of the door	أَمَامَ ٱلبَاب
inside/in the house	بِالبَيْت / فِي البَيْت
in it 'f-m'	فِيهَا/ فِيهِ
in the college	فِي ٱلكُلِّيَّة
in/inside the elevator	فِي ٱلمَصْعَد
in the long run	عَلَى ٱلمَدَى ٱلبَعِيْد
in the school	فِي ٱلمَدْرَسَة
in the university	فِي ٱلجَامِعَة
I say to him/to her	أقولُ لَهُ / لَـهَا
on/above the chair	عَلَى/فَوقَ ٱلكُرْسِيّ

on/above the table	عَلىٰ/ فَوْقَ ٱلطَّاوِلَة
on top of everything	فَوْقَ كُلِّ شَيْء
to the back	إِلىٰ ٱلوَرَاء
to the college	إِلىٰ ٱلْكُلِّيَّة
to the front	إِلىٰ ٱلأَمَام
to the school	إِلىٰ ٱلْمَدرَسَة
to the university	إِلىٰ ٱلجَامِعَة
to whom it may concern	إِلىٰ مَن يَهُمُّهُ ٱلأَمْر
until we meet again	إِلىٰ ٱللِّقَاء
under the bed	تَحْتَ ٱلسَّرِير
until the morning	حَتَّىٰ ٱلصَّبَاحِ
and until the evening	وَحَتَّىٰ ٱلمَسَاء
with the father and the mother	مَعَ ٱلوَالِد و ٱلوَالِدَة
with my friend 'm'	مَعَ صَدِيقِي
with my friend 'f'	مَعَ صَدِيقَتِي
with the pencil	بِـالقَلَم

Notes:

Appendix 13: Commonly Used Particles

Adverb	Conjunction	Interrogative	Negative
around حَوْلَ	and وَ	what مَا	not مَا
before قَبْلاً	when عِنْدَما	who مَن	will not لَن
between بَيْنَ	since مُنْذُ	to whom لِمَن	is not لَيْسَ
close by قَرِيباً	until/up to حَتَّى	what مَاذَا	never لا أَبَداً
during أَثناءَ	then, thereupon ثُمَّ	when مَتَى	except him/her عَدَاهُ/عَدَاهَا
far away بَعِيداً	where حَيْثُ	where to إلى أَيْنَ	without بِلَا
inside دَاخِلَ	or أو	how كَيْفَ	is not/do not لا
sometimes أَحْيَاناً	If لَو	why لِمَاذَا	none/ no one, not even one لا أَحَداً/ولا واحِداً
through خِلالَ	but لَكِن	for what لِمَاذَا	not-except him/her مَاعَدَاهُ/مَاعَدَاهَا
without, set aside دُونَ	as/similar/like مِثلَ	how much كَمْ	have not/don't have. مَاعِنْدِي

Notes:

Appendix 14: Answers for Arabic vocabulary puzzles 1-1 to 8-1

Puzzle #1-1

						١أ	
ن	ي	ن	ث	إ	ل	٢ل	
					ب		
		ي	ت	ا	ق	ي	د	٣صَ
					ت		
ن	ي	ر	ا	م	٤ت		
٦نَ				٥أ			
ق				خ			
رَ				بَ			
أُ				ا			
ةُ				ر			

ACROSS

2-٢ Monday

3-٣ My friends 'fp'

4-٤ Exercises

DOWN

1-١ The house

5-٥ News

6-٦ We read it

Puzzle #2-1

ACROSS

1-١ Street

6-٦ He read 'past'

7-٧ Students

8-٨ An hour, a watch

9-٩ She writes

10-١٠ Notebook

DOWN

2-٢ A bird

3-٣ They eat

4-٤ A team

5-٥ Professor

Puzzle #3-1

ACROSS

4-٤ I say

6-٦ Yes

7- ٧ Father

10-١٠ Children

11-١١ Mothers

12-١٢ Annoyed 'f'

DOWN

1-١ Sad 'f'

2-٢ We learn

3-٣ The lesson

5-٥ Friends, companions

8-٨ Girls

9-٩ Happy 'f'

319

Puzzle #4-1 (__ References two-word vocabulary)

ACROSS

1-١ Welcome
3-٣ Where are you 'm-f,p'?
6-٦ My sister
7-٧ They play
8-٨ Exam
11-١١ We are honored by you 'f'
12-١٢ I eat chicken
13-١٣ An Arab
14-١٤ An Indian
15-١٥ I read a book
16-١٦ He
17-١٧ University student
18-١٨ Those are engineers

DOWN

2-٢ My friend
4-٤ With me
5-٥ He works
9-٩ House
10-١٠ He says

Puzzle #5-1

ACROSS

2-٢ Happy
3-٣ Went out
4-٤ Graduated
5-٥ College
6-٦ He writes
7-٧ This
8-٨ Pencil
9-٩ He runs away
10-١٠ I eat
11-١١ He heard
13-١٣ Worked
15-١٥ He
16-١٦ Who
20-٢٠ How much
21-٢١ Or
22-٢٢ Uncle (maternal)
23-٢٣ Thereupon

DOWN

1-١ My companion 'm'
12-١٢ Engineering
14-١٤ Library
17-١٧ Brothers and sisters
18-١٨ He wrote
19-١٩ He read 'past tense'

Puzzle #6-1

ACROSS
- 3-٣ He is happy
- 4-٤ We hear
- 6-٦ He erased
- 7-٧ He goes out
- 9-٩ They advance 'm'
- 11-١١ He delays
- 13-١٣ He laughed

- 1-١ He runs
- 2-٢ He sleeps
- 5-٥ He takes
- 8-٨ We
- 10-١٠ You 'f'
- 12-١٢ You eat 'f'
- 14-١٤ They help

DOWN
- 15-١٥ They travel
- 16-١٦ They watch
- 17-١٧ They work
- 18-١٨ They
- 19-١٩ She
- 20-٢٠ They Listen
- 21-٢١ They study

- 22-٢٢ They memorize
- 23-٢٣ They thank
- 24-٢٤ We go away
- 25-٢٥ He studies
- 26-٢٦ She studies

Puzzle # 7-1

ACROSS
5-٥ They
6-٦ Tree
8-٨ She
9-٩ Room
10-١٠ Window
13-١٣ Door
14-١٤ Building floors
16-١٦ College
19-١٩ Professor
22-٢٢ Schools
23-٢٣ Stars
25-٢٥ Sun
26-٢٦ Moon
27-٢٧ Sky

DOWN
1-١ Cars
2-٢ Streets
3-٣ Stores
4-٤ Buildings
7-٧ Offices
11-١١ Virus
12-١٢ Corona
15-١٥ Computer
17-١٧ City
18-١٨ States
20-٢٠ Center
21-٢١ Vaccine
24-٢٤ My mother
25-٢٥ Father

Puzzle #8-1 (─── References two-word vocabulary)

ACROSS

2-٢ University
3-٣ Classes
4-٤ Office
5-٥ An employee
6-٦ Laboratory
7-٧ Languages
9-٩ Soccer (two words)
10-١٠ Field
11-١١ Games
13-١٣ Teacher 'f'
14-١٤ A language
17-١٧ A player
20-٢٠ Far away
21-٢١ Close by
22-٢٢ Names, nouns

DOWN

1-١ Student
8-٨ Our factories
12-١٢ Workers, laborers
15-١٥ Coffee
16-١٦ Sciences
18-١٨ Sugar
19-١٩ Tea

List of Recommended Resources

Al Munjid, Arabic-Arabic Dictionary, 20th edition, Dar El-Mashreq Publishers, 1969.

Ba'albaki, Munir. *Al–Mawrid: A modern English Arabic Dictionary.* Dar El-Ilm Lil – Malyeen Publishing, 1973.

Cowan, J M., editor. *The Hans Wehr Dictionary of Modern Written Arabic,* 3rd edition, Spoken Language Services, 1976.

Doniach, N S., editor. *The Oxford English – Arabic of Current Use,* Oxford University Press, 1972.

Wortabet, Johan and Porter, Harvey. *Arabic – English Dictionary,* Hippocrene, 1993.

Gaafar, Mahmoud and Wightwick, Jane. *Arabic Dictionary and Phrasebook English - Arabic , Arabic – English,* 12th edition. Hippocrene, 2009.

Tuite, Simon, senior editor. Bilingual Visual Arabic English. Dorling Kindersley, 2009.

Gaafar, Mahmoud and Wightwick, Jane. Easy Arabic Reader, A three-part text for beginning students. McGraw Hill, 2011.

Hezi Brosh and Lutfi Mansur. Arabic Stories for Language Learners, Traditional Middle Eastern Tales in Arabic and English. Tuttle Publishing, 2013.

Textbooks

Alsaeed M. Badawi,, et al. *AlKitaab Al Assasi Fii Taleem ul-lugeati-l-Arabia for Non Speakers of Arabic, Part 2.* Arabic Organization for Education, Culture and Science. Tunis. 1987.

(الكتاب الأساسي في تعليم اللغة العربية لغير الناطقين فيها ، تأليف السعيد محمد بدوي، محمد حماسة عبد اللطيف ومحمود البطل . المنظمة العربية للتربية والثقافة والعلوم . تونس ١٩٨٧)

Abdul-Rauf, Muhammad. *Arabic for English Speaking Students,* 6th edition. Al-Saadawi Publications, 1996.

Brustad, Kristen, et al. *Al-Kitaab Fii Ta Allum Al-Arabiyya.* 3rd edition. Georgetown University Press, 2011.

Frangieh, Bassam K. *Arabic For Life.* Yale University Press, 2012.

Brustad, Kristen, et al. *Alif Baa: Introduction to Arabic Letters and Sounds,* 3rd edition, Georgetown University Press, 2015.

Arabic Media Websites

Al-Jazeera, http://www.aljazeera.net/portal.

Al – Arabiya, http://www.alarabiya.net/.

BBC Arabic, http://www.bbc.com/arabic.

Arabic Media, http://arabic-media.com/arabicnews.htm

Arabic App

ArabGPT ذكاء اصطناعي عربي, Artificial Intelligence App https://www.arabgptapp.com/